Growing up in the **PEOPLE'S CENTURY**

MY
DAD'S
AT THE
FRONT

Where is yours?

Growing up in the
PEOPLE'S
CENTURY

JOHN D. CLARE

BBC BOOKS

Based on the BBC TV series PEOPLE'S CENTURY
Executive Producer: Peter Pagnamenta

Consultant: Rona Selby
Designer: Judith Robertson
Editors: Mike Hirst and Kate Petty
Picture researchers: Maria Chambers and Frances Topp
Maps: Peter Bull

Published by BBC Children's Books
a division of BBC Worldwide Limited
Woodlands, 80 Wood Lane, London W12 OTT

First published 1996
Text by John D. Clare © BBC Children's Books

ISBN 0 563 40410 8

Colour reproduction by Radstock Reproductions Ltd, Midsomer Norton
Printed by Cambus Litho Ltd, East Kilbride
Bound in Great Britain by Hunter & Foulis Ltd, Edinburgh
Jacket printed by Lawrence Allen Ltd, Weston-super-Mare

Contents

The People's Century

IT WAS NOT JUST the start of a new year. It was the start of a new **century**.

In Russia, Alexander Briansky saw it happen! He was 17 years old. He remembers the parties:

'There were fireworks. There was drinking. There were crowds on the streets – nobody stayed at home. People started hugging, kissing, making friends and making resolutions. We had huge hopes.'

Alexander Briansky is still alive. He has lived through the whole of the twentieth century.

There has never in the history of humankind been a century like the twentieth century. It has changed the world – completely, and for ever. It has been a century of prosperity, freedom, marvels and miracles. And it has been a century of hunger, heartbreak, terror and evil.

What must it have been like for children growing up in the twentieth century? What was it like to live through these amazing times?

In this book, the children of the twentieth century will tell you.

Stanislava Kraskovskaya
a Russian woman,
born in 1897

"In my century we've had electricity, trams, cars – right up to astronauts. This is my century.

"It's been fascinating."

In this poster, drawn for a French car company, the new world meets the old world head on.

△ This French cartoon of 1901 imagined an age of traffic jams in the skies.

◁ The new century gave people hope for the future. This piece of music celebrated the start of a new age, when inventions would change the world.

1900–1918

A World of Hope

IN 1900, people thought that education and science would make the world a better place. In the United States, politicians promised 'a square deal for every man and every woman'.

Visitors to the Paris Exhibition of 1900 saw steam engines and machine tools – the triumphs of the past. But the real attractions were the marvels of the age to come – a moving pavement, cinema and electricity.

▽ Fifty million people visited the Paris Exhibition of 1900.

▷ Wonders of the exhibition: a German motor car and an American typewriter – inventions that would change the world.

Raymond Abescat
Paris, France, 1900

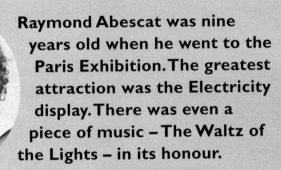

Raymond Abescat was nine years old when he went to the Paris Exhibition. The greatest attraction was the Electricity display. There was even a piece of music – The Waltz of the Lights – in its honour.

"At home we used oil lamps and candles. We didn't have electricity. So here was this whole exhibit devoted to electricity. It was wonderful to see the building all lit up in the evening.

"On the right, before you reached the exhibition, there was also a big wheel. You would get into a little cabin and bit by bit you would see the whole exhibition from your cabin on the wheel. Things would go wrong every now and again – the wheel would break down and you'd be stuck in mid-air!

"The other great curiosity was a moving walkway which had been built in one part of the exhibition. Sometimes, people who didn't understand how it worked would make complete and utter fools of themselves by falling off as they tried to get on!"

Beryl Bristow
America, 1900

Not everyone was convinced, however, that electricity was the energy of the future.

"In 1900 my father was building a house … so we asked the head of the Company, which we should put into the house, gas or electricity, and he said, 'Oh, gas, by all means. Electricity's just a fad; it'll never last.'

"So that's what we got."

The Sky's the Limit!

IT FLEW for only 12 seconds. It travelled barely 37 metres. But on 17 December 1903, Orville and Wilbur Wright's plane, Flyer I, made the world's first-ever powered flight. Technology gave people hope for the future. Flight was its most exciting achievement. Now, literally, the sky was the limit!

▽ Blériot, the first pilot to fly across the English Channel, became a national hero. Even the little woolly pom-pom hat he wore when he flew became popular.

▽ Flyer I makes its maiden voyage in 1903.

Jeanne Plouvin
France, 1909

The new technology developed quickly. On 25 July, 1909, a Frenchman called Louis Blériot became the first person to fly across the English Channel. Schoolgirl Jeanne Plouvin saw him take off:

"It was quite an event. When we knew that Blériot was going to leave, all of us children in the district, everyone from the youngest to the oldest, gathered in a field . . .

"The corn had been harvested, and so there we stood in this cornfield, behind some oil drums, because they didn't let us get too close. It would have been too dangerous . . .

"He was an engineer, a gentleman, very daring, because he knew he was risking his life . . .

"We heard the engine rumble. He taxied forward, took off gently, and then was gone. Everyone clapped. Everyone shouted. We cried 'Bravo! Bravo!' . . .

"There was immense joy when we heard that he'd landed in England. 'Blériot has made it,' they shouted in the street. Everyone was happy. It was a victory for France."

Ecstatic supporters welcome Blériot as he arrives in Dover.

A World of Contrasts . . .

IF THE WORLD OF 1900 was a world of hope, it was for most people a world also of dull work, hunger and hardship.

Even in Europe, the average length of life was only 46 years. There was little or no help for the homeless or sick.

Outside Europe, things were worse. Dorah Ramothibe, a black South African, worked for a white farmer who beat her and kicked her. If she wanted to speak to him, she had to crawl towards him on her knees, clapping her hands.

For some, the years before 1914 were *La Belle Époque* – 'the beautiful time'. But, says Jeanne Plouvin: 'The *belle époque* was for the rich: people who could dress well and eat well – while the workers got nothing but stewed grease and gristle. It wasn't the *belle époque* for everybody.'

△ The motor car was one of the new century's most exciting developments – if you were rich.

▷ The cities of the United States bustled with activity. Its workers were the highest paid in the world.

◁ For most people – particularly those who lived in Africa or (as in the picture) Asia – life was a never-ending struggle simply to survive.

...and Oppression

IN 1900, FEW PEOPLE had rights, freedom or a say in their government.

Many countries were part of the empires of the European nations – 290 million Indians, for instance, were ruled by 5,000 officials from Britain.

Other countries were ruled by an autocrat (a 'sole ruler'). In China, the ruthless Manchu emperors ruled a quarter of the world's population.

Even in the so-called 'democracies', many people had no vote. In the United States many blacks were scared they would be killed if they tried to vote.

◁ Women who campaigned for the right to vote were called 'suffragettes'. In 1900, only in New Zealand could women vote in national elections.

▽ Huge areas of the world were 'colonies' in the empires of the European nations.

Britain

France

Belgium

Portugal

Germany

The Netherlands

Sergei Butsko
Russia, 1903

Russia was ruled by the Tsar of Russia. He was an autocrat. There was no parliament. Political parties were illegal.

Most of Russia's 90 million peasants faced lives of hardship and hunger. They lived in poverty, so that others could live in luxury.

Sergei Butsko was born in 1896.

"My sister and I collected stones in the landowner's fields and put them into piles so that they would not cause problems during the ploughing and harvesting.

"Half the population lived in awful poverty. The landowner of our district lived in Warsaw. He spent all his time going to parties. Every so often he'd show up on his land to collect his money. Then he'd shoot off back to Warsaw."

A New Life

BETWEEN 1900 AND 1914, thirteen million people emigrated from Europe to the United States: the greatest voluntary migration ever. Most were poor. Many were Jews, escaping from persecution in Russia and Poland.

To these people, America was 'paradise!' – the chance to make a better life – and they sang for joy when they saw the Statue of Liberty.

▽ Young immigrants arriving at Ellis Island in New York.

▷ A poster advertising sailings from Ireland to the United States. Doesn't the sea look calm!

GREAT SOUTHERN AND WESTERN RAILWAY OF IRELAND.

DOMINION LINE

ROYAL AND UNITED STATES MAIL STEAMERS

1900.—PASSE

Nellie Gillenson
New York, 1910

Some poor people could afford tickets only for their children, who were put on a boat and sent to relatives in the New World.

Nellie Gillenson was sent to a new life in America.

"I'll never forget the goodbye of my mother. She was squeezing me and I was squeezing her ... People wanted to pull me off of my mother and my mother didn't let me go ... But I never saw my mother or father again.

"The first step I made on the ground of America, I felt like I wanted to kiss it, and I said: 'God bless America'."

▷ Most emigrants went to the United States, but others went to Brazil and Argentina in South America.

◁ Not everyone who wanted to emigrate was successful. When immigrants arrived in the USA, each had a medical inspection. Only healthy people were allowed to stay.

Striking Out

IN THE YEARS between 1900 and 1914, workers in western Europe no longer accepted that they had to do as they were told. They went on strike for better wages and conditions. Some strikes became very violent.

The workers won shorter working hours, workers' insurance schemes, better housing, better schools and old age pensions.

▷ Workers were stronger when they joined together, so they formed trade unions. This is a membership certificate of the British National Union of Railwaymen.

▷ It was normal for people to be working full-time before they were teenagers. They worked long hours for low wages.

◁ In 1905, there was a wave of strikes and riots in Russia. These child workers are on strike in Odessa, in southern Russia.

The Tsar was forced to grant the people a parliament, called the Duma.

Minnie Way
Scotland, 1911

Minnie Way had to go to work at the age of 12, because her father had died. From the age of 13, she worked a ten-hour day.

She remembers a strike in 1911, and the strikers' song, which went to the tune of 'Jesus loves the little children'. The strikers were demanding a wage rise of ten per cent:

"I was working in a jute factory when I was 12 years old. I did a day at work and a day at school until I was 13, and then my mother applied for a full-time extension ... Conditions were hard in the working class ...

"That strike went on for six weeks – yes, six weeks exact, and we'd go down the streets singing – what was it now?

We are out for higher wages,
As we have a right to do.
But we'll never be content,
'Till we get the ten per cent,
For we have a right to live
as well as you."

The Great War

ON 28 JUNE 1914, Archduke Franz Ferdinand, the heir to the throne of Austria-Hungary, was shot and killed in Sarajevo. It was the event that sparked off the First World War.

In the years leading up to 1914, many people had begun to feel that war was inevitable. Most people were nationalists. Nationalists believed in national pride, power and empire. They thought that other nations were their enemies.

All over Europe, arms factories turned out weapons. In France, Blériot's factory made aeroplanes for the military. Twenty-five million soldiers were trained and kept 'in reserve', in case of war.

To try to prevent a war, governments made treaties of alliance with other states. But in 1914, these alliances dragged them into war.

Austro-Hungarian politicians blamed the small country of Serbia for Franz Ferdinand's death. Austria-Hungary declared war on Serbia. Russia came to Serbia's help. Germany entered the war to help Austria-Hungary, and attacked Russia's ally, France. When the German armies went through Belgium, Britain declared war on Germany.

Everyone was excited. They thought that the war would be glorious, and that it would be over by Christmas. They were terribly wrong.

The Great War became the first world war. Fighting took place all over the world. The war involved 70 million men from 20 countries. Troops from Africa, India, Australia, New Zealand and America came to Europe to fight – and die – in a conflict they knew hardly anything about.

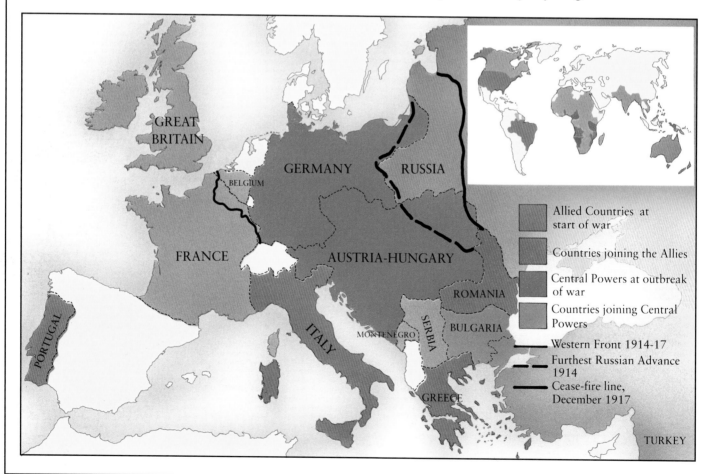

GREAT BRITAIN
GERMANY
RUSSIA
BELGIUM
FRANCE
AUSTRIA-HUNGARY
ROMANIA
PORTUGAL
ITALY
SERBIA
BULGARIA
MONTENEGRO
GREECE
TURKEY

Allied Countries at start of war

Countries joining the Allies

Central Powers at outbreak of war

Countries joining Central Powers

Western Front 1914-17

Furthest Russian Advance 1914

Cease-fire line, December 1917

Ted Smout
Australia, 1914

Ted Smout was 17 years old and still at school when war was declared in 1914. He joined the army for a variety of reasons. (White feathers were the mark of a coward.)

Australia has promised Britain **50,000** MORE MEN WILL **YOU** HELP US KEEP THAT PROMISE

"In Australia at that time we were part of the British Empire and were very loyal to Britain, and we felt it was our war ... Apart from which, if you stayed a year or two longer, you'd have got a white feather from the girls!

"No, it was the thing to do."

Karl von Clemm
Germany, 1914

Karl von Clemm lists some of the confused reasons which led a young man to go to war:

"All over the world there are young fellows who say: 'The war's just an adventure, and it's our country' – and it's patriotism, and partly to get medals – it's a mix.

"And it's wonderful because you get away from family and all of a sudden you're on your own at 18 or 19 or 20, which is great."

▽ German women wave goodbye to their menfolk, leaving for the Front in 1914.

Trench Warfare

THE GERMAN ARMY marched quickly into France. But by September 1914, the advance had been stopped. Instead of retreating, the Germans dug trenches. So did the French and the British. Soon there was a system of trenches running from Switzerland to the English Channel.

At first, the generals tried to break through enemy lines, but it was almost impossible to get across the 'No Man's Land' between the two lines of trenches. To advance, soldiers had to move forward on foot, with a rifle and bayonet. The trenches they were attacking were defended with machine guns. An attack usually resulted in thousands of casualties.

In 1916, at the battle of Verdun, the Germans did not try to break through. They just killed as many French soldiers as they could. The battle lasted ten months. In all, 315,000 French soldiers died – but 282,000 Germans died killing them.

▽ A typical British trench in the First World War. To fire at the enemy, the soldier stands on the firestep. Duckboards on the floor of the trench stop soldiers sinking into the mud.

◁ Warfare was mechanised. The weapons of war were machines. They killed with the tireless precision of a machine. A machine gun could fire 600 rounds a minute.

The battle of the Somme in 1916 went on for 141 days and claimed over a million dead. The war became a 'war of attrition', in which both sides just tried to wear down the enemy.

Trenches filled with water. Sometimes men drowned in the mud. Occasionally, they trod on the bodies of the dead so they wouldn't get stuck. Rats grew fat on the flesh of the dead. The air was filled with the smell of blood and rotting bodies. Lice gathered in the seams of clothes.

Deserters were executed. The only way out of the war was to be wounded, or to go mad.

△ Big guns were used to bombard the enemy's positions before an attack. More soldiers were killed by shells than by anything else.

▽ Both sides used poison gas in the war. Phosgene gas blinded the victims, burned their skin and ripped out the lining of their lungs. It was a very painful way to die.

The War Effort

THE FIRST WORLD WAR was the first 'total war'. The armies at the front needed weapons, ammunition, food and uniforms. The war turned into a battle of industrial production. Britain blockaded German ports. German U-boats sank British merchant ships.

Governments tried to keep up war hatred by propaganda, accusing the enemy of atrocities.

▷ Women took over men's jobs in the factories. They drove buses, fought fires, delivered coal and did a hundred other jobs.

▽ Women were a vital part of the war effort. Here, teenage girls fill shells with explosive.

THESE WOMEN ARE DOING THEIR BIT

LEARN TO MAKE MUNITIONS

Hermine Venot-Focké

France, 1916

Hermine Venot-Focké was 13 when war broke out. Her mother was a singer who went to the hospitals to sing to wounded men:

"The thing that moved me most happened in a hospital in Drancy. There was a young lad in bed, who looked no more than 18 . . . He'd been dying for two days, waiting for his mother.

"I sat with this boy, feeling totally overwhelmed with grief. It was terrible. But he must have felt that there was a woman beside him because he stretched out his poor hands, which I took in mine . . .

"I was so overcome that I thought, 'He's waiting for his mother and I'm going to give him the kiss he's waiting for.' It never crossed my mind to ask what his name was. I never forgot him.

"I kissed him, and he died."

Soldiers and their families kept in touch by writing, but even postcards were censored by the Army. Most men could not bring themselves to tell their families what life on the Front was really like.

Armistice

AFTER THREE YEARS of slaughter, human despair and mud, the troops' morale began to fail. In 1917, a number of French regiments mutinied.

On the Eastern Front, the Russian Army was in even worse shape. In 1917 the soldiers disobeyed their commanders and went home.

Also in 1917, America entered the war. Four million young Americans signed up to fight in Europe.

The Germans tried to win the war by making a huge attack before the Americans could arrive. At first they advanced quickly, driving back the exhausted French and British troops.

But in August 1918 their attack failed.

The German Army had not been defeated, but the German people were

▽ The USA enters the war in 1917.

◁ German submarine attacks on American merchant ships sailing to Britain and France were a major factor in bringing the United States into the war in 1917.

△ A poster asking Russians to buy war bonds. All governments needed money to pay for the war. The Russian Government collapsed under the strain of the war effort.

living on berries and potatoes. Germany asked for peace. An Armistice (ceasefire) was agreed at 11 a.m. on 11 November 1918.

Germany was ruined. North-east France lay in ruins. Russia was in revolution. Austria-Hungary and the Turkish Empire had fallen apart. Nine million soldiers were dead. Millions more were physically or mentally wounded. The war had cost so much, and had solved nothing.

1918–1933

A Peace Which Failed

'I HOPED AND FELT that this was the end of war for all time.'

Many people shared British soldier Walter Hare's hopes that the end of the war would bring about a better world. Woodrow Wilson, the American President, agreed with them. In December 1918, he came to Paris for the Peace Conference. He said that he wanted a 'just peace'.

Some people, however, were not so forgiving. Nine million people had been killed in the war. France lay in ruins. Many people in France and Britain wanted revenge.

◁ Woodrow Wilson wanted nations to solve their problems by talking, not by war. He wanted democracy, and self-determination (the right of peoples to govern themselves).

▽ Many Germans were angry at the 1919 Peace Treaty. This cartoon shows Poland as a wolf, stealing land from Germany, dressed as Little Red Riding Hood.

Karl Nagerl

Germany, 1923

Reparations ruined Germany. In 1923, prices rose by 1400 per cent; this is called 'hyperinflation'. A pound was worth 20 trillion marks. People picked up their wages in laundry baskets.

Karl Nagerl was a schoolboy:

"We were out playing football and one of my friends said: 'I'm going to the shop to buy a couple of bread rolls.' He had a 500,000 mark note . . .

"But he only came back with one, because a roll now cost 400,000 marks."

The Germans were not allowed to take part in the Peace Conference. In June 1919 they were told to go to Versailles, near Paris, to sign a Peace Treaty. Its terms were harsh. It said that Germany was to blame for starting the war. Germany's colonies and German lands in Europe were taken away. Germany could not have a navy or an air force.

Above all, to repair the damage of the war, Germany was told to pay vast 'reparations', in instalments lasting until 1988.

The Germans were furious. In the end, the Peace of 1919 did not solve the First World War; it helped to cause a second.

▷ In Germany in 1923 paper money was worth so little that it was cheaper to play with bank notes than to buy building bricks!

A New World

THE PEACE TREATIES which ended the First World War tried to make a new world.

New countries were created. The old empires of Germany and Russia lost land. Austria-Hungary was dismantled. Instead, new nation-states came into being, such as Poland and Czechoslovakia. In 1919, the independent kingdom of Yugoslavia was created around the old Serbia. It united many of the Slav peoples of southern Europe.

Also in 1919, the League of Nations met for the first time. Its aim was 'Peace by Reason' – for nations to settle their differences by talking about them. It supported disarmament and tried to defend weaker countries against the strong. Unfortunately, aggressive leaders like Mussolini and Hitler just ignored it.

▽ The Peace Treaties of 1919 changed the map of Europe.

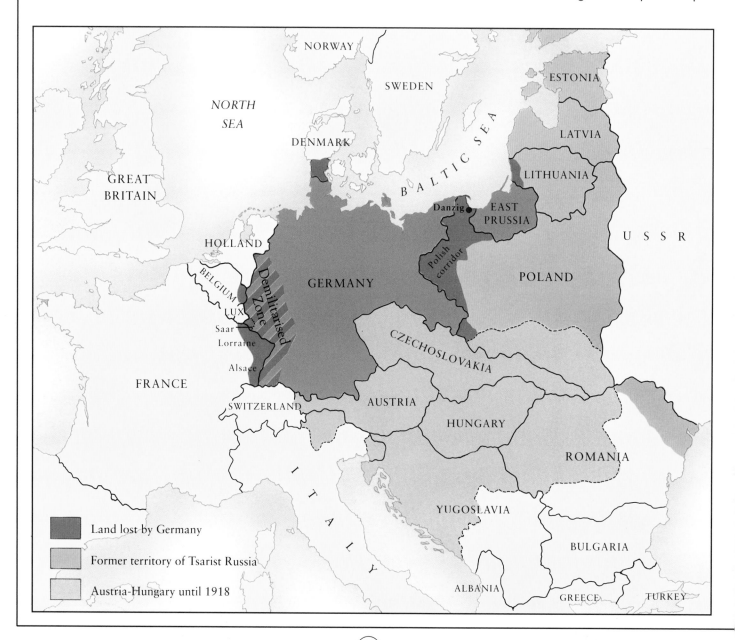

NORWAY

SWEDEN

NORTH SEA

DENMARK

GREAT BRITAIN

BALTIC SEA

ESTONIA

LATVIA

LITHUANIA

Danzig

EAST PRUSSIA

U S S R

HOLLAND

BELGIUM

LUX

Saar

Lorraine

Alsace

Demilitarised Zone

GERMANY

Polish corridor

POLAND

FRANCE

SWITZERLAND

CZECHOSLOVAKIA

AUSTRIA

HUNGARY

ROMANIA

I T A L Y

YUGOSLAVIA

BULGARIA

ALBANIA

GREECE

TURKEY

Land lost by Germany

Former territory of Tsarist Russia

Austria-Hungary until 1918

Anna Masaryka
Czechoslovakia, 1919

The first president of the new republic of Czechoslovakia was the Czech politician Tomas Masaryk. Anna Masaryka, his grand-daughter, remembers the excitement and emotion of those days.

"There were many, many people, all screaming, cheerful, embracing each other ... [I noticed that my mother was weeping.] I asked 'Why do you weep — everybody is so happy,' and she said the only words: 'We have freedom'."

▽ Many young people believed fiercely that the League of Nations was 'the dawn of a new era' in world politics. Millions signed a petition, asking the nations to reduce the number of their weapons.

△ Poland had not existed as an independent state since 1795. In 1919, the famous pianist Paderewski became the President of the new republic of Poland.

The Red Flag

'TAKE TO THE STREETS, RISE UP . . .
Forge happiness for the world,
End the bowing and scraping.
Go boldly! Shine! Rejoice!'

In 1917, Alexander Briansky was one of the people who took part in the Russian Revolution.

The First World War had ruined Russia's economy. In the towns, people were starving. In February 1917 huge crowds took to the streets. The soldiers sent to crush the rioters joined with them. The Tsar was forced to abdicate.

A provisional government tried to bring in a few reforms. But the Russians wanted more. They wanted 'peace, land and bread' and a say in the government. Councils of workers and soldiers – called the 'Soviets' – grew up in the cities. Many Russians became Communists – they did not believe in private property, and wanted the workers to rule the country.

But only one group promised the people 'peace, land and bread'. They were the Bolsheviks – the most extreme Communists. Their leader was Lenin. Many young people such as Alexander Briansky joined the Bolshevik Army – the Red Guards.

△ Children look at the fallen head from a statue of the Tsar. At first, the Tsar's family were kept under house arrest, but in July 1918 they were executed by the Bolsheviks.

In October 1917 the Red Guards seized control of St Petersburg, the capital city of Russia. Lenin took control of the government. A new state called the Soviet Union had been created.

◁ On 25 October 1917, Red Guards captured the Winter Palace, the headquarters of the provisional government.

▷ This Soviet poster portrays Lenin as the workers' leader.

Building the Revolution

'OUR HEARTS are so joyful. In no other country are there such happy young people as us.'

The Russian Revolution gave Tatiana Fedorova – and many other Russians – hope for 'the victory of Communism all over the world'. They believed that there would be no more rich and poor, only goodness and noble behaviour.

The Communist Government took land from the old landowners and gave it to the peasants. It took control of the factories. It built hospitals and schools. In 1920, it announced that every Russian would be taught to read and write.

In 1924, Lenin died, and Josef Stalin came to power. He launched the Five-Year Plans – schemes to develop Soviet industry.

▽ The Five-Year Plan. Keen young Communists endured terrible conditions building factories, furnaces and power stations.

△ The Soviet Government passed laws to make women equal with men in jobs and pay. Soviet girls could join the volunteer workers' organisation Komsomol when they were 14.

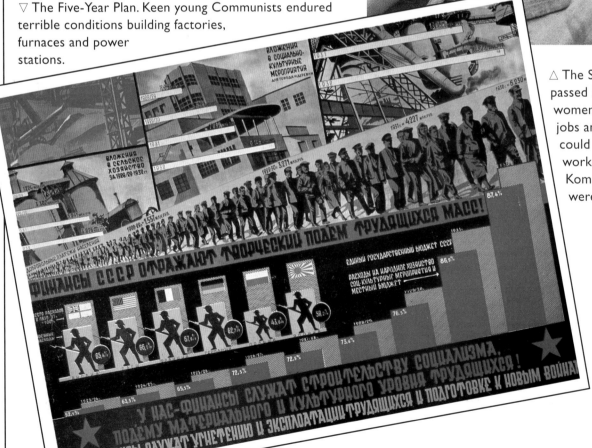

Anastasia Denisova
Soviet Union, 1924

When she was 17, Anastasia Denisova went out teaching people to read.

"We went from house to house in search of illiterate people. We made a note of their names. We then found suitable rooms to hold classes in.

"I met a young woman with a child who didn't know what she could do with her baby.

"I said: 'Here's a text book for you. You'll learn to read. I'll come to your house . . .' She held the baby in one arm, and sat and wrote while she rocked him. She studied so keenly. I'll remember that for ever."

Ella Shistyer
Soviet Union, 1923

Communism appealed most to young people. Ella Shistyer was a student.

"When Lenin said that Communism is Soviet power plus electrification, I decided that I should become an electrical engineer, that that was my holy duty . . .

"And I didn't want to just draw up plans. I wanted to build an electric power station. That was my mission and I achieved it . . .

"The revolution gave me the right to feel equal to any man. It gave me the right to work, to study what I wanted to study."

▽ The Communists sent special propaganda trains (called agit-prop trains) out into the countryside to spread their political ideas. This boy is taking part in a play about the benefits of Communism.

Socialism in Practice

STALIN WANTED to revolutionise Russian agriculture. He abolished the old ways of farming. Each village was reorganised into a 'collective' farm. The peasants' land and animals were taken over by the State. They were told to share their machinery and tools.

The results were disastrous. The richer peasants – the 'kulaks' – hated collectivisation. Rather than hand over their animals, many peasants killed them. Less food was produced, not more.

Stalin was furious. The kulaks' homes and possessions were confiscated. Seven million kulaks were put to death. Stalin took all the peasants' grain – including the seed for next year's crop – and used it to feed workers in the towns. The result was a terrible famine; in some villages the whole population starved to death.

As time went on, Stalin became a monster. He boasted: 'Our factories are run without owners . . . Our fields are worked without kulaks. The people are in charge.' But behind the scenes, his blood-lust ran wild. Quotas were drawn up telling local party officials how many 'traitors' they had to find and execute. He often insisted that they found more traitors than they were supposed to.

▷ The Government encouraged people to hate the kulaks. In this children's story, kulaks and factory owners try to pull up a prize turnip for themselves. The turnip turns out to be a Red Army soldier who blows them away!

▷ Perhaps seven million people died during the famine. Many children were orphaned or died of starvation.

Pelagaya Ovcharenko

Ukraine, 1932

Pelagaya Ovcharenko's parents died during the famine of 1932. Government officials came to deal with them:

"Three people came into the house. One tended the horses. Two were piling up corpses on the cart.

"They threw on my mother. They threw on my father. My father gestured to me. The man said: 'He's almost ready; he's almost dead.'

"When my father gestured to me I knew I had to go and hide. The men swore but they couldn't find me because I'd crawled away on my hands and knees and hidden myself.

"The men took the cart to a big hole and tipped the bodies in, regardless of whether they were dead or alive."

The Great Escape

FOR MANY YOUNG PEOPLE in the West, the pace of the 1920s and 30s was fast and furious.

The first movies were shown in 1895, in Paris. The 'flickers' were shown as part of Music Hall programmes and were just pictures of everyday life. Before long, however, huge audiences were paying to see dramas and comedies.

Before the First World War, movies were made in 25 different countries. Gradually, however, Hollywood began to take over. Directors learned new techniques such as the close-up. In 1927, Al Jolson's film, *The Jazz Singer*, was the first 'talkie'. Cinema became big business.

Movie actors became stars. Charlie Chaplin boasted that he was a star in places that had never heard of Jesus Christ.

People began to model their lives on the film stars. Films taught young people how to smoke a cigarette, how to do their hair, how to kiss. In America, in 1922, the Hays Commission was so alarmed by the effect films were having on young people's morals, that it laid down rules about how actors could behave on film. It did not allow nudity or 'excessive kissing'. Its most famous rule was that a man and woman could never share a bed on screen – even if they were supposed to be married – unless the man had one foot on the floor.

◁ Shirley Temple made her first film when she was four, and she won a special Oscar when she was just six years old.

▷ Radio was another popular form of entertainment in the 1920s and 1930s. It was the success of radio which forced film-makers to develop synchronised sound ('the talkies').

Harold Lloyd was a successful star of early silent comedies. His movies always included hair-raising stunts which he performed himself.

Before the Talkies

EARLY MOVIES were shown in black and white. They were 'silent movies' (they had no soundtrack). Because the cameras were turned by hand, the number of frames per second varied – which is why actors' movements often seem jerky or speeded up.

The poor quality of early film meant that everything – even scenes which were set indoors – had to be filmed outdoors.

OCTOBER 25c
CLASSIC
A BREWSTER PUBLICATION

◁ Rudolf Valentino was the hero of a number of romantic silent movies. Magazines such as *Classic* gave readers information about their favourite stars.

▽ The Keystone Cops first appeared in 1913. They rarely solved a crime, but their amazing stunts and slapstick comedy always made the audience laugh.

POLICE PATR

POLICE DEPT.

Danny Patt

Maine, United States, 1924

The early silent movies were accompanied by a pianist.

Danny Patt began playing the piano in a cinema when he was just 12 years old. It was not quite as glamorous a job as it seemed:

"You had to have a good repertoire of mood music, such as hurries, chase music, battle music, fight music, Indians and cowboy music, marches and all that sort of thing ... Between my sister and me we collected a lot of music and I was able to find enough so that I could do a pretty good job of cueing the first movie. After that the job was mine.

"Every character had his or her own theme. This is still done today in modern movies. Most every movie has a theme song that's played all the way through, whenever the lovers appear, but I used to find a tune that would fit each character. In *Way Down East*, for instance, there were several comic characters. For the old maid aunt, I used a theme called Humoresque by Tchaikovsky.

"When the light came on for intermissions, all the young kids used to throw peanuts at me. I struggled not to show my annoyance, because if I did then they'd really pelt them!"

▽ A cinema pianist accompanies the film, *Mabel's Dramatic Career*. Caption frames told the audiences what the actors were saying – though the man turning the hand-cranked projector found he had to slow down at that point, to give his audiences time to read the words. Films were most popular with children and poor people, and many of them could barely read.

The invention of the Talkies put all the cinema pianists out of work.

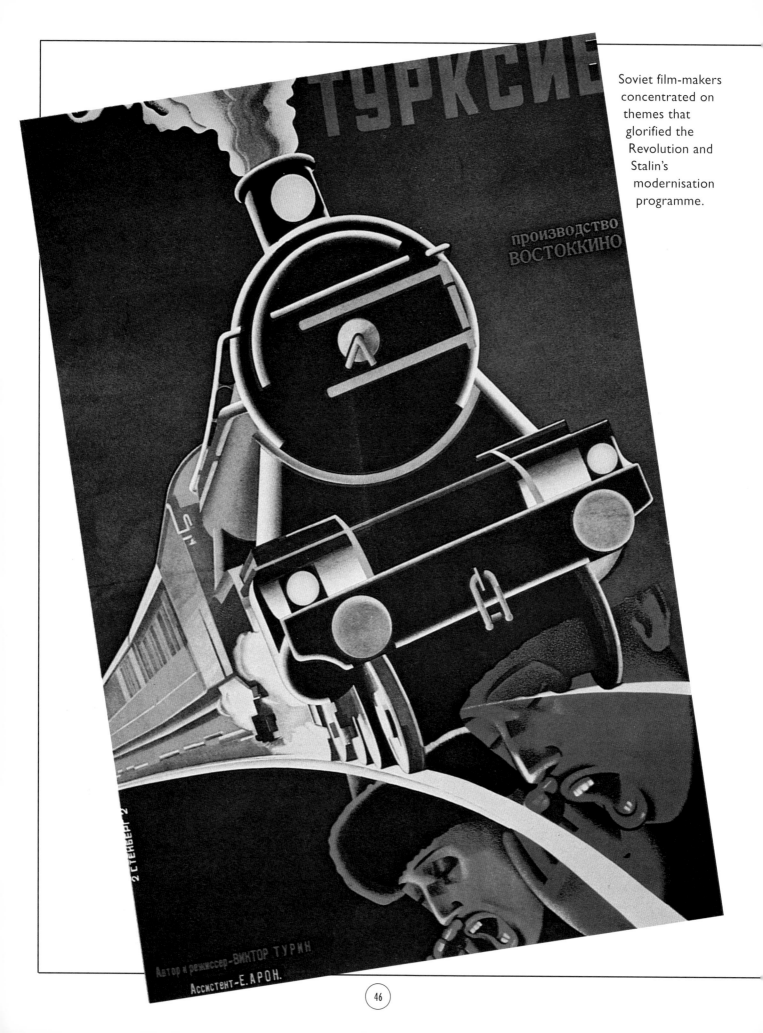

ТУРКСИБ

производство
ВОСТОККИНО

2 СТЕНБЕРГ 2

Автор и режиссер–ВИКТОР ТУРИН
Ассистент–Е. АРОН.

Soviet film-makers concentrated on themes that glorified the Revolution and Stalin's modernisation programme.

The Power of the Silver Screen

BY THE 1930s, 25 million British people went to the cinema every week. At that time, the population of Great Britain was 46 million.

The cinema became a source of news and information, as well as of entertainment. British and American cinema-goers watched newsreels telling them about the unemployed and the economic depression.

In Fascist Italy, Nazi Germany and the Communist Soviet Union, the Governments realised that the cinema had the power to affect the way people thought. They began to make propaganda films, to indoctrinate as well as entertain.

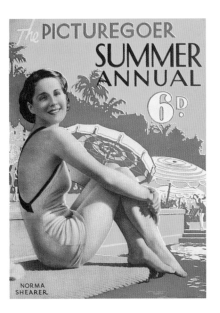

Orietta Salvadore
Italy, 1938

An Italian schoolgirl, Orietta Salvadore, was convinced by one of the films turned out by the Fascist Government – even though members of her own family had been imprisoned by the Fascists.

"I remember the film, *Luciano Serra – Pilot*. It was about a pilot who was a great man because he succeeded in killing the enemy. He was good because he killed so many people. He was a Fascist – a real man because he was a Fascist. The film told me that with men like him we would win the war.

"When I went home, my family told me: 'You enjoyed watching that film, but think about how many people are in prison because they don't agree with it.'"

△ The cinema was 'the great escape'. It gave people the chance to forget the drab, uneventful poverty of their own lives, and dream of something more glamorous.

▷ The Nazis were experts at film propaganda. Leni Riefenstahl's film, *Triumph of the Will*, was about the 1934 Nazi rally at Nuremberg.

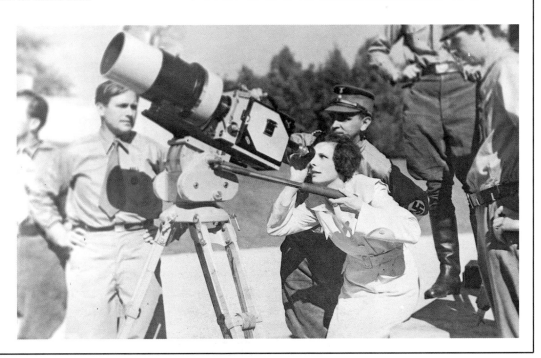

Sporting Fever

THE OLYMPIC GAMES OF 1908 were a turning point in Olympic history. They were the first games where competitors took part as members of a national team. The American tug-of-war team even accused the British team of cheating!

Like the cinema, sport offered poor people an escape from their humdrum lives. It gave them excitement, and a sense of belonging. Boxing was one of the first sports to attract huge audiences. Soon bicycle racing, baseball, rugby, tennis, cricket and soccer were popular all over the world.

Inevitably, sport soon became an international issue. When Uruguay played Argentina in the 1930 Soccer World Cup, it led to a breakdown of diplomatic relations. When English cricketers used 'body-line' fast bowling in the Test Series of 1933 between Australia and England, the ensuing controversy damaged trade between the two countries.

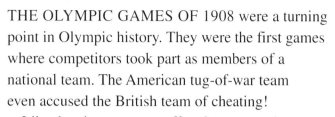

The RING
25 CENTS   JUNE

MAX SCHMELING
The Heavyweight Comeback King

SPECIAL PICTORIAL NUMBER

◁ Many people played sport during the 1920s and 1930s; golf was attractive to wealthy people.

△ Successful sportsmen and women became heroes. They were the stars of songs, magazines, children's comics and cigarette cards.

WILLS'S CIGARETTES

△ When Max Schmeling, from Nazi Germany, fought the black American Joe Louis for the heavyweight boxing title of the world in 1936, it carried the hopes of millions of people. For America's blacks, when Louis was defeated, it was 'like a great president had died'. In 1938, Joe Louis won the rematch, in the third minute of the first round.

▷ Schoolboy Bill Pethers had just found out that he was to be a ball boy for the British FA Soccer cup final.

Rooting for the Yankees

Anna Freund

New York, United States, 1928

Anna Freund was born Anna Daube in New York in 1917.

In America, baseball was the great popular sport. Anna and her sisters were big fans – or 'rooters' – for the Yankees baseball team.

"We had three ball teams in New York City . . . The loyalties of the fans were just phenomenal, if you were a Dodger rooter, you were a Dodger rooter. If you were a Yankee rooter, you were a Yankee rooter. Unfortunately my brother-in-law married into our family as a Dodger rooter – so he had a very sad time for a while, being adjusted to us. But he got adjusted.

"I think the atmosphere at the ball games was very, very exciting. You had great times rooting, you could say almost anything you wanted. You never heard

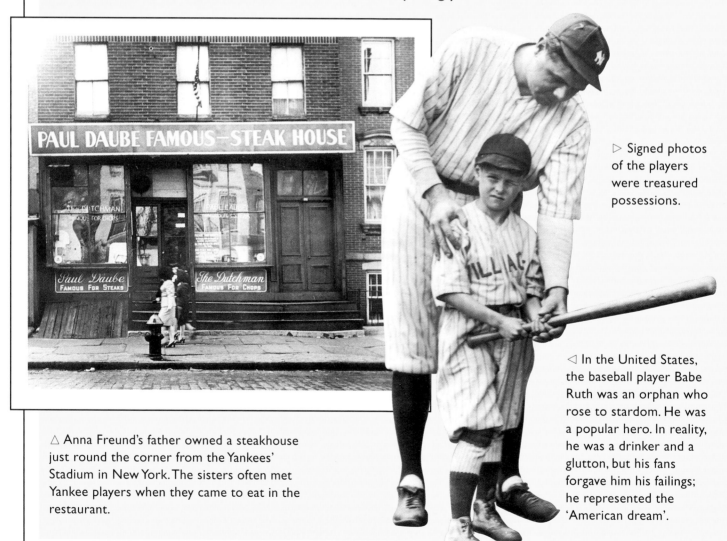

△ Anna Freund's father owned a steakhouse just round the corner from the Yankees' Stadium in New York. The sisters often met Yankee players when they came to eat in the restaurant.

▷ Signed photos of the players were treasured possessions.

◁ In the United States, the baseball player Babe Ruth was an orphan who rose to stardom. He was a popular hero. In reality, he was a drinker and a glutton, but his fans forgave him his failings; he represented the 'American dream'.

In the 1920s and 1930s, the magazine *Tip Top Weekly* contained baseball stories.

anything said that was very vulgar – you might call an umpire 'a bum'.

"We would go to the ball games rather than the movies. And the way we were punished was to say, 'You can't go to the ball game'. Lou Gehrig was one of my favourite players. I was heartbroken when he got married – I was thirteen or fourteen years old . . .

"My father said that I knew everything about the ball players except the number of teeth they had."

Mass Production

'IT WASN'T THE SAME every day. Sometimes it would be almonds. Sometimes just cherries . . . It did vary.' Maybe – but the life of biscuit factory workers in the 1920s really doesn't sound very interesting!

They could have blamed Henry Ford (left) for their boring jobs. Ford was an American car manufacturer who tried to find new methods of production to get his car workers to produce more, faster.

First, he carefully timed the workers' actions. Often, it was possible to double a worker's output, simply by saving wasted effort. Then Ford split up the task of making a car into hundreds of different jobs. Each job was done by a different worker, who did nothing else all day.

Finally, in 1913, Ford set up the first assembly line. A conveyor belt carried the car shell from one worker to the next, while a complicated system of overhead pulleys carried the parts to the workers. Ford built the largest car factory in the world – the River Rouge Plant at Detroit. Coal, rubber and iron flowed in at one end of the factory; 168,220 black Model T Ford cars a year drove out of the other.

The plant employed 80,000 men.

◁ Every Model T Ford car produced in any one year was exactly the same. Ford said that people could buy it in 'any colour so long as it was black'. In 1916, about a third of all cars in America were Model Ts.

▷ Mass production not only produced vehicles such as this Fiat bus, but also paid the workers high enough wages to buy their own cars.

On the Line

ASSEMBLY LINES were soon used to make other products – such as gramophones, radios, furniture and clothes. Prices went down, but profits went up. So did wages – workers earned enough to be able to afford to buy the cars they made. In this way, mass production led to mass consumption.

But the work was terrible. To keep up, the worker had to work like a machine himself. By the 1930s, car workers were angry and demoralised. They formed trade unions and fought the employers. In America in 1932, four Ford workers were shot and killed in riots.

▷ By the late 1920s, shops were selling cheap, mass-produced, 'off-the-peg' clothes.

The 1936 film *Modern Times* starred Charlie Chaplin as a confused worker, caught in the cogs of the machine he had to mind. Many assembly line workers knew how he felt.

Charles Hill
England, 1922

At the age of 14, Charles Hill went to work for the Vulcan car works, who were proud to say that they still made their cars slowly, by hand.

"There were skilled men there . . . who were there all their life to their dying day, all skilled craftsmen in their own sphere. In the body shop, there was a lot of wood framing of the motor car body, and then there was the panel beating . . . it was done with hammers . . .

"You were walking down the road, and you'd see these cars, cars that you'd actually worked on, people riding in cars, and it gave you an ego."

Giovanni Gobbi
Italy, 1926

Giovanni Gobbi went to work at the Fiat company when he was 15. Fiat's owners had copied Ford's production techniques.

"In the beginning the assembly line was run by hand, worked by the men. Later they motorised the line with a chain . . .

"One day my boss put a stopwatch in my hand and said: 'Go and time how long it takes to do that job.'

One of the first people I had to time was a man who could have been my grandfather . . . The poor man was working away and I was a young kid having to time him. It was awful.

I couldn't do it and asked for a different job."

In Fascist Italy, trade unions were banned, but companies offered workers' clubs and a certain amount of social security. Fiat workers' children could join a Fiat youth movement rather like the Boy Scouts.

The Depression

THE 1920s were a boom time in the United States. The prices of shares on the American Stock Exchange (on Wall Street in New York) rose rapidly.

Many Americans gambled their savings to buy shares, hoping to make a profit.

But on 24 October 1929, there was a financial panic. Share prices fell . . . and fell . . . and fell. People called it the 'Wall Street Crash'.

A million Americans were ruined.

Business confidence collapsed. All over America, people stopped buying things. As a result, companies went bankrupt. They sacked their workers. But then the growing millions of unemployed people also stopped buying. More firms went bankrupt.

The effects of the Crash were felt all over the world. When American firms stopped buying copper, Chilean copper miners were thrown out of work. No ships were needed because there was no trade – so British ship-builders lost their jobs.

△ When the shipyard at Jarrow, in the north-east of England, closed down, three-quarters of the working population of the town was unemployed. In 1936, they marched to London to ask the Government to help. The Government refused.

◁ People were ruined by the Wall Street Crash.

$100 WILL BUY THIS CAR MUST HAVE CASH LOST ALL ON THE STOCK MARKET

Yvonne Mouffe

Belgium, 1932

Yvonne Mouffe was a coal miner's daughter. Her father lost his job when he took part in a strike against wage cuts. She watched a film of her family, taken at the time:

"There were nine children in the family. My father worked in the mines, but during the strike he was earning nothing. We slept on the floor. Some slept in the table with straw, the others on the floor.

"That's me in the cradle, because I'm ill. My father turned the table round, otherwise there wouldn't have been enough room to sleep on the floor ...

"We ate nothing but potatoes ... that's all we were given. How did we live like that?"

▷ Chile exported nitrates (used for fertilisers and explosives) to the United States. When demand fell, thousands of Chilean nitrate workers lost their jobs.

In countries with no state welfare services, people starved. Yet at the same time, farmers were throwing away food. People were too poor to buy it. For ordinary people, the Depression was devastating.

In America, they joined in long 'breadlines', queuing for a mug of soup and a hunk of bread. The song summed it up:

'Can't get no work, can't draw no pay.
Unemployment getting worser every day.
Nothing to eat and no place to sleep –
All night long folks walking the street.
Doggone – I mean the panic is on.'

The New Deal

PEOPLE WANTED their Governments to do something to end the Depression. But Governments seemed powerless. They said the Depression was inevitable. The people's reply was to say that there was 'something rotten with the whole system'. There were riots and marches. Many looked to Communism to answer their problems. It was a time of danger for democracy. In Italy, the Fascist dictator Mussolini had already seized power in 1922. In Germany, in 1933, Adolf Hitler took over the Government.

But in America, in 1932, Franklin D. Roosevelt was elected as President. His theme music was 'Happy Days are Here Again', and he promised the American people 'a New Deal'. In the first 100 days of his presidency, he set up a number of major schemes to get Americans back to work. The biggest project – the Tennessee Valley dams – provided water and electricity for eight states. Thousands of workers were employed through Roosevelt's schemes. These workers spent their wages – which helped to get the economy going again.

△ In Sweden, the Government tackled unemployment in the same way as the Americans, setting up state schemes to put people to work.

▽ These men are employed to mend the road by the Works Progress Administration – a Government agency set up under the New Deal.

USA WORK PROGRAM WPA

Loye Stoops

United States, 1933

The Depression affected the countryside just as much as towns. The worst-hit areas were in the southern states, where farmers fought against low prices for their crops and a long drought which made their land impossible to farm. Loye Stoops' family were among the many poor farmers helped by the New Deal.

"We stayed in Oklahoma for about three or four years after the drought began. We planted crops but dust storms would come and then there was nothing but sand. We kept trying to farm until the waterhole level dropped and there was no water in the wells. Then President Roosevelt came on the scene, which was a blessing. He would pay the farmers $30 or $35 for a cow because there were so many cattle and not enough hay or water . . . it would take a wagon almost to carry $35 worth of food!"

Loye's family moved to California.
"My husband was working on the WPA and he would have enough money every month to buy one plank. We started in with the floor and four planks up. I don't know how many months it took till we got to the top."

Franklin D. Roosevelt meets poor farmers in 1932.

1933–1945

Hitler's Germany

'NO STATESMAN HAS ever been as loved as Adolf Hitler was then.'

That is how Luise Essig, once a Nazi education officer, remembers Hitler's Germany in the years 1933-39. For her, it was a time of happiness and joy: 'Ah, it's all flooding back to me now. Those were happy times.' And it is true that, for all those Germans who were not the Nazis' targets, life was happy.

The Nazis came to power in Germany in 1933. Their leader, Adolf Hitler, did not win an election. He was given power as part of a political deal – and then immediately made himself a dictator.

△ Burning books. Hitler would not allow any opposition or ideas other than his own. He abolished all rival political parties. He abolished trade unions. He threw his opponents into concentration camps.

Before Hitler, Germany had been in a state of crisis. Germans felt they had been humiliated by the Peace Treaties which ended the First World War. Thirty per cent of the work force was unemployed.

Hitler set up public works schemes to provide jobs. He ignored the Treaty of Versailles and built up Germany's armed forces. 'After 15 years of despair, a great people is back on its feet,' he claimed.

Most of all, Hitler gave Germany hope. Germans were told that they were the Master Race, and that it was their destiny to rule the world. Heinrich Himmler, one of the Nazis' leaders, assured them: 'We march according to eternal laws. We are on the way to a distant future.'

It was a belief that dragged the whole world to disaster.

▷ Young people, particularly girls, were always placed at the front of Nazi rallies. It made the Nazis look like 'the party of youth'. Also, their enthusiasm added to the general atmosphere of hysteria.

▽ The SA (*Sturmabteilung*), formed by Hitler to beat up his opponents, parade at Nuremburg in 1933. The German people were thrilled by the ceremony, the flags and – most importantly in a time of despair and chaos – by the sense of hope and discipline.

Hitler's Youths

WHY DID ORDINARY, caring German people support a man as evil as Adolf Hitler?

Most Germans never saw the horrors of Nazi Germany – the concentration camps, the murders, the medical experiments. All they were told, over and over again, was that life would be happy if they lived 'for Führer and Fatherland'.

It was the young Germans who most easily fell under the spell of Nazi propaganda.

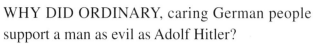

ALLES LIEBE UND GUTE

KOMM ZU UNS!

DEUTSCHES JUNGVOLK
IN DER HITLER-JUGEN

Herausgeber: Reichsjugendführung der NSDAP.

△ Children were taught to think of Hitler as a kindly father-figure.

◁ (Far left) A propaganda poster for the Hitler Youth.

◁ A typical Nazi stereotype: a fit, beautiful, fair-haired girl from the RAD (the National Labour Service) cheerfully brings in the harvest.

Hanne-Lore Lügering
Germany, 1930s

Hanne-Lore Lügering watched an old film of the May Day celebrations in the village of Rettner in Germany. She remembered how she felt about the Nazi Young Girls' League youth organisation.

"I was six . . . We put up a swastika. I liked wearing the Young Girls' uniform. I loved the Hitler Youth organisation . . . Blond, blue-eyed, tall people were much admired. They were the flag carriers . . . Ilse carried the flag because she was pretty, tall and blonde."

Ilse Woile
Germany, 1930s

Ilse Woile also watched the film of the May Day celebrations.

"There I am. I'm carrying the flag. I was very proud to carry the flag. My main thought was that I'd be in the film."

Herta Grabarz
Germany, 1930s

Young Germans were not evil. They were attracted to the fun.

"We weren't swept along. We took part because everybody did. We didn't want to be left behind, so we went along with it."

▷ Dedicated: members of the Hitler Youth listen carefully in 1933.

An Aryan Nation

NAZI SCIENTISTS CONCOCTED theories to prove that Germans were a superior race. Nazi historians invented a glorious German past, and Nazi archaeologists dug up bogus relics to prove it.

The Nazis wanted to establish an ideal race: the Aryan race. SS officers who wanted to marry had to prove pure German blood as far back as 1750. The Government gave loans and medals to persuade Germans to have more children.

Germany's Jews were the main victims of this theory. Germans were told that Jews were inferior. 'These Jewish subhumans have filled Europe with criminals,' complained a typical newsreel of the time. All Germany's problems were blamed on the Jews. Slowly but surely,

△ 'Racial research': measuring 'Jewish' features.

people began to accept what they were told. Nazi propaganda made sure that nobody tried to stop what followed. The Nazi Government began to persecute the Jews. Jews were forbidden to be doctors or lawyers. They were forbidden to marry Germans.

Gradually, the persecution grew. Jewish shops were covered with racist graffiti. Jews were humiliated by being forced to scrub pavements. Then, on 9 November 1938, Jews all over Germany were attacked. Three hundred Jews were killed and 1,000 synagogues were burned down. The event was called Kristallnacht (crystal night), after the broken glass that covered the streets in Jewish areas.

▷ The aftermath of Kristallnacht.

The story-book *The Poisonous Mushroom* taught children to hate Jews.

The Second World War

HITLER'S FOREIGN POLICY was aggressive. First, he united all the German-speaking people of Europe by taking over Austria and the Sudetenland in Czechoslovakia (1938).

Then he began to seek 'living space' in other countries. In 1939 he marched into the rest of Czechoslovakia. Finally, in September 1939, he attacked Poland. Britain and France declared war.

The Nazis quickly conquered Poland; Britain and France could do nothing to help. Then, after a short lull, Hitler struck west. Just as quickly, he conquered Holland, Belgium and France. The Allied forces were powerless to stop the Nazi Blitzkrieg (lightning war), which involved fast attacks using aeroplanes, tanks and armoured cars. Britain fought alone until the summer of 1941, when Hitler invaded Russia.

Nazi Aggression 1935-1940

NORWAY
April 1940

FINLAND

SWEDEN

ESTONIA

DENMARK
April 1940

LATVIA

EIRE

GREAT
BRITAIN

LITHUANIA

EAST
PRUSSIA

HOLLAND
May 1940

GERMANY
March 1935
build up of armed forces
November 1938
attacks on Jews

POLAND
September 1939

BELGIUM
May 1940

LUX

CZECHOSLOVAKIA
March 1939

Sudetenland
October 1938

FRANCE
May 1940

AUSTRIA
March 1938

HUNGARY

SWITZERLAND

ITALY
November 1936
Hitler's Ally

ROMANIA

SPAIN

YUGOSLAVIA

German Stukas returning from an air raid.

The People's War

FROM THE START of the Second World War, civilians were also involved in the struggle to win. Women were needed to fill places in the factories left by men who had gone to fight. It was punishingly hard work, but many women enjoyed the independence of working life.

◁ A member of the Hitler Youth delivers the mail.

▽ In Britain, people expected a war of air raids and poison gas.

Horst Westphal
Hamburg, 1941

Children also were expected to 'do their bit'. Although he was a schoolboy, Horst Westphal worked for the German war effort, collecting meat bones to help make explosives.

"We used to ring the bell and greet them smartly at the door – 'Heil Hitler: do you have any bones?' . . . Next day we took the bones to school and handed them in."

△ In Britain, many children were 'evacuated' from the towns to country villages, where they would be safer. Each evacuee was given a label for identification.

▷ The British Government encouraged the population to grow more food and 'dig for victory'.

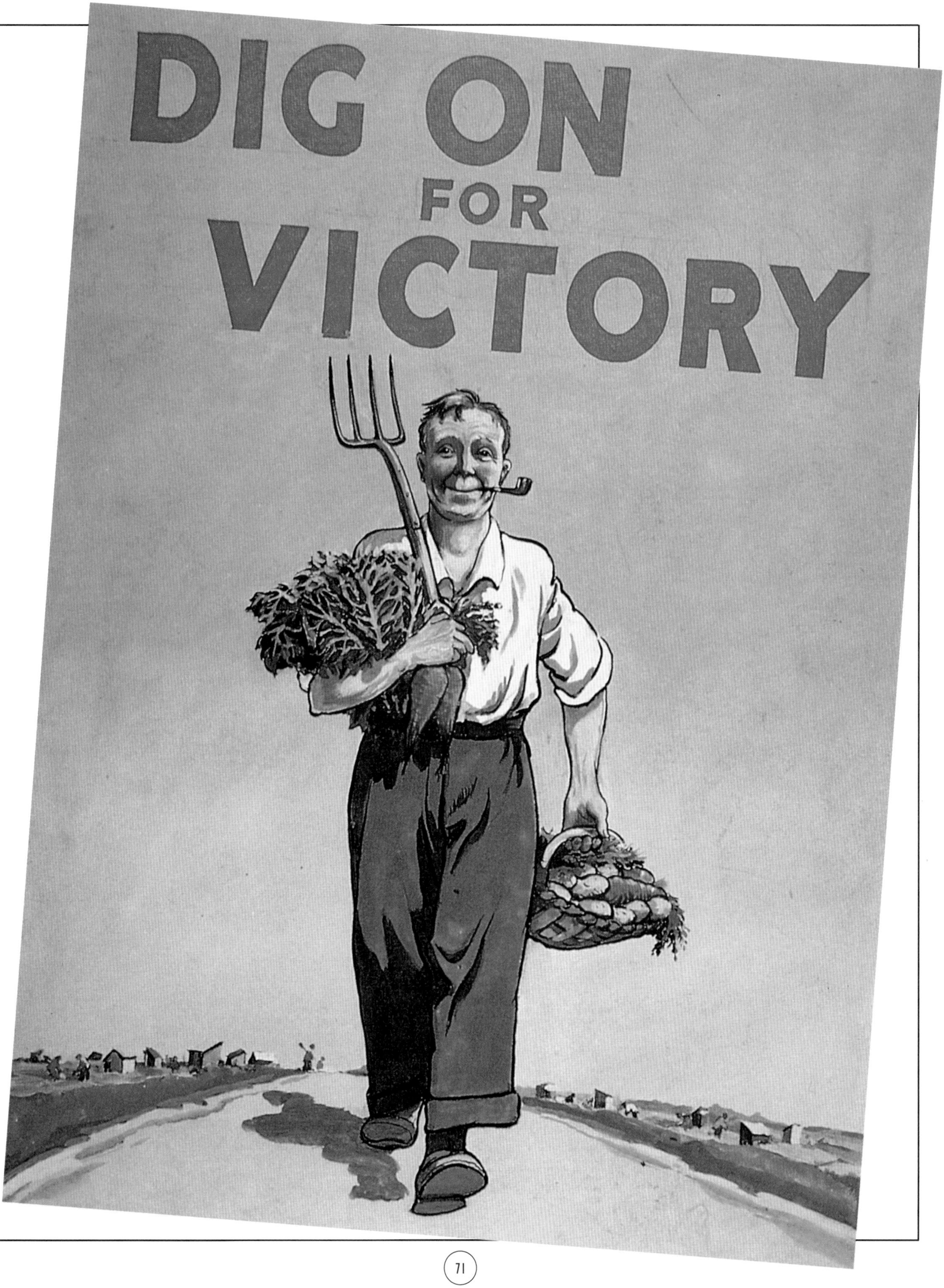
DIG ON
FOR
VICTORY

The Measure and . . .

IF CIVILIANS were working for their country's victory, then they were also targets. The war between the Nazis and Britain became a war of bombing raids.

First, Hitler tried to break the morale of the British by a bombing campaign – 'the Blitz'. Night after night, as the bombs fell, British townspeople were forced to sleep in makeshift shelters at the bottom of the garden. In London, people sheltered in the Underground railway stations.

The British were not broken. Their Prime Minister, Winston Churchill, spelt out their mood of revenge: 'We will mete out to the Germans the measure, and more than the measure, they have meted out to us.'

For the moment, however, Britain had to bear the terror of the Blitz.

Sid Newham
Plymouth, 1941

Plymouth was the most densely bombed city in Britain, because it had an important naval dockyard. Over 1,000 people were killed, and 3,000 injured. Young Sid Newham was one of those who, at night, fled to the fields to escape the attacks.

"We went up on the moor because we were scared stiff, and we used to snuggle down among the hedges. I'd get my little sister to snuggle into me on one side, my brother on the other side, and the bombs would start dropping. Then you could see the sky starting to light up, and you'd think: 'What part of town is it this time?'"

◁ The Blitz

▽ Bomb damage in the East End of London in 1941.

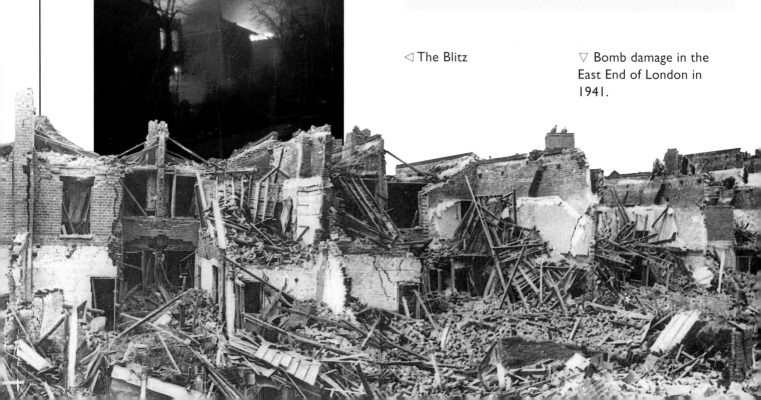

. . . More than the Measure

IN 1941, the United States had entered the war, and the Nazis were forced onto the defensive (see page 78). Allied bombers carried out huge raids over Germany. Ninety per cent of houses in German towns were damaged or destroyed.

On 27 July 1943, over the city of Hamburg, the RAF dropped more bombs – and killed more people – in one night than the Nazis had during the whole of the Blitz. The bombs created a firestorm. Air temperatures reached 1000°C. Winds of 120 m.p.h. lashed the city. Perhaps 42,000 people died. Hamburg was utterly destroyed.

Margarete Zettel
Hamburg, 1943

Although she was only a teenager, Margarete Zettel was a Civil Defence worker in Hamburg. During the raid, she rescued six babies from a blazing building, for which she won a medal.

"It was an inferno. Pure chaos. There was an unbelievable stench. The next thing we noticed was the disgusting smell. I still have it in my nostrils now. Blood, mortar. Everything was burning. The mixture was absolutely gruesome . . .

"I brought the last child out, thank God, and immediately the burning stairs behind me collapsed . . .

"My hair was burnt off, right up to the edge of the steel helmet I was wearing."

The Holocaust

'THIS ISN'T THE SECOND WORLD WAR. THIS IS THE GREAT RACIAL WAR.'
Herman Goering, in charge of Nazi propaganda

WHEN WAR BROKE OUT in 1939, Hitler blamed the Jews. War, he warned, would result in 'the destruction of the Jews in Europe'. Jews were rounded up and crowded into ghettos (areas where only Jews lived). There, they were allowed to die of disease and starvation.

Eventually, the 'final solution' to the Jewish 'problem' was put into practice: the whole Jewish race was to be exterminated.

▷ In 1940, 400,000 Polish Jews were put into the ghetto – a tiny slum area in the centre of Warsaw. They could not leave. Most had only a bowl of soup a day to live on. By 1943, only 60,000 were alive. They rebelled. The Nazis had 2,000 trained soldiers, tanks, artillery and flame-throwers. The Jews had 12 guns, a few pistols and home-made bombs. But it took the Nazis four weeks to put down the rising.

When the fighting was over, all those Jews not killed were sent to the gas chamber.

Zvi Michaeli
Ejszyszki, Lithuania

Zvi Michaeli was 16 years old when a Nazi death squad came to his village.

"When we all undressed – when I saw Rabbi Zushi undressed I thought this was the end. The verses from the Psalms which he recited in our ears: up to then I'd been confident that we wouldn't die.

"And my father was saying: 'You will live. Don't be afraid. You will live and take revenge.' He put his left hand on me. I saw my brother David climbing up his thigh, so tight. He clung so tight. He didn't let go of him until the last minute.

"And the shots of the machine gun. There was a mixture of voices, of people crying, and children, and the shots, and the dust, and everything mingled together.

"I found myself inside the pit. I felt my father give me a push, and then fall on top of me. He covered me. He wanted me to live."

Arriving at the
death camp
– Auschwitz.

Disaster in Russia

IN JUNE 1941, Hitler invaded Russia. At first, Nazi forces made great gains against the Russian armies, and Nazi soldiers captured village after village. Faced with prisoners they regarded as subhuman, their officers declared, 'The normal rules of war need not be followed.' Sometimes they shot all the men and burned the village to the ground. Sometimes they sent the men and the healthy women back to Germany as slave workers, then drove the old women and children out of the village to fend for themselves.

In the end, however, Hitler's invasion of Russia ended in disaster. The Nazis were defeated by the vast size of Russia and by the Russian winters. At the sieges of Stalingrad and Leningrad, the Nazis suffered defeats from which they never recovered.

Twenty million Russians died in the Second World War.

▽ A Soviet war poster. The Russians hated the Nazis.

▷ Hitler's fatal mistake. The Nazis invade Russia, 1941.

Lubov Zhakova

Leningrad

The siege of Leningrad lasted two and a half years. Food ran out; in the end the Russians were making bread from wood cellulose and sawdust, and soup from glue. Three-quarters of a million of the inhabitants died from starvation, cold and disease. At the height of the siege, Dmitry Shostakovich, composer and a city fire warden, wrote a symphony. It was performed as a symbol of defiance.

Amazingly, despite the siege, one of the inhabitants of Leningrad had managed to grow some flowers. At the end of the symphony his niece, Lubov Zhakova, gave them to the conductor.

"I was pushed into the middle and there was nothing else for me to do but to present the flowers. And there was a note inside them. I still remember it to the last word: 'With gratitude for preserving symphonic music'. We were overcome most of all by a feeling of celebration and grandeur; joy that we would be victorious."

Enter the United States

UNTIL 1941, the Nazis were winning the war. After 1941, however, the tide began to turn.

The Japanese attack on Pearl Harbor in 1941 brought the United States into the war – and all the resources of US industry. America declared itself the 'great arsenal of democracy', supplying all the Allied armies with the weapons to fight the Nazis.

△ An American B17 'Flying Fortress' bomber.

▽ Pearl Harbor, 1941. Japanese planes launch a surprise attack on the American navy base.

▷ 'Rosie the Riveter'. As more American women joined in war production, attitudes towards women began to change. There were still beauty contests, but the women were judged by their job records and attendance as well as their looks.

Total War

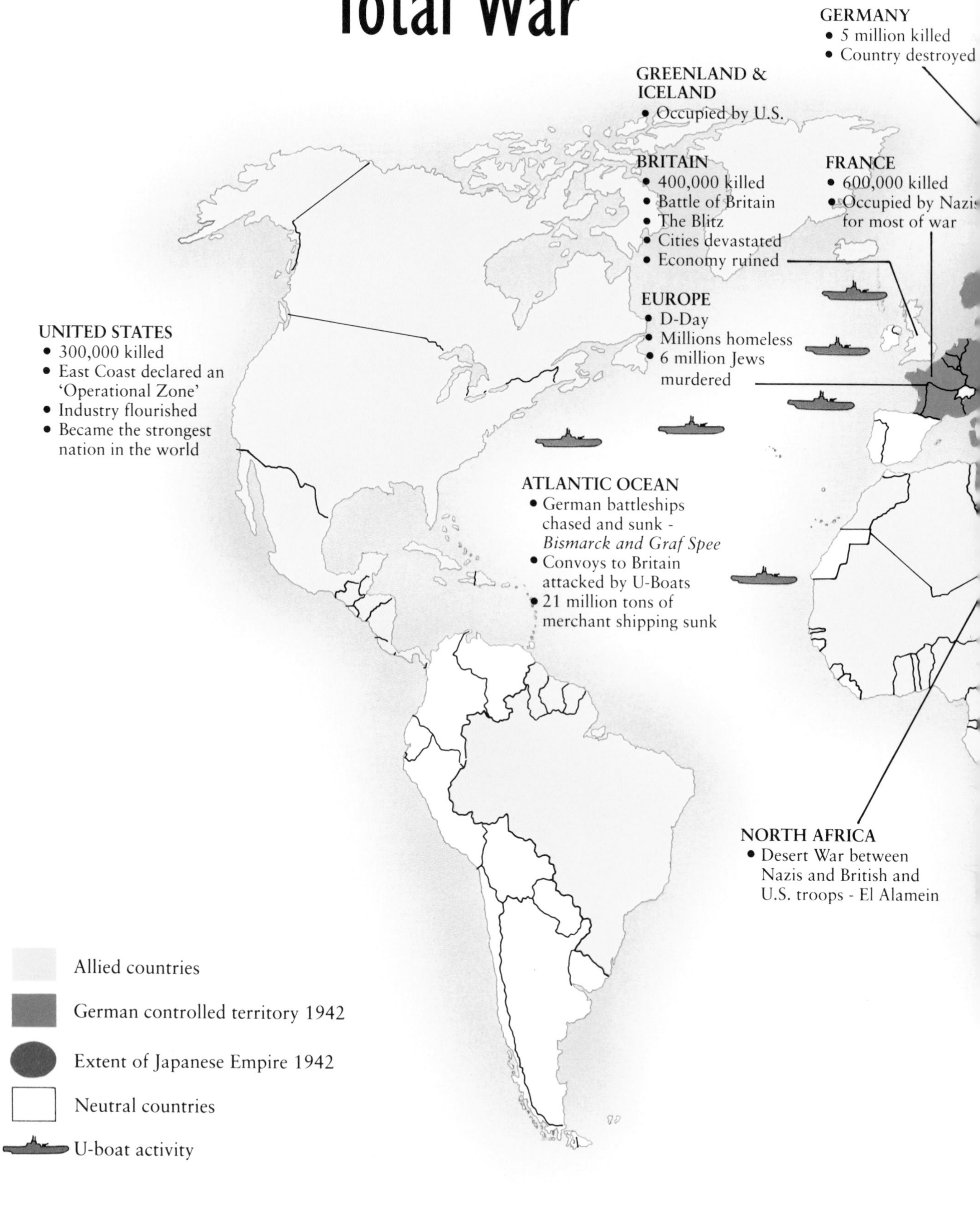
GERMANY
• 5 million killed
• Country destroyed
GREENLAND & ICELAND
• Occupied by U.S.
BRITAIN
• 400,000 killed
• Battle of Britain
• The Blitz
• Cities devastated
• Economy ruined
FRANCE
• 600,000 killed
• Occupied by Nazis for most of war
EUROPE
• D-Day
• Millions homeless
• 6 million Jews murdered
UNITED STATES
• 300,000 killed
• East Coast declared an 'Operational Zone'
• Industry flourished
• Became the strongest nation in the world
ATLANTIC OCEAN
• German battleships chased and sunk - Bismarck and Graf Spee
• Convoys to Britain attacked by U-Boats
• 21 million tons of merchant shipping sunk
NORTH AFRICA
• Desert War between Nazis and British and U.S. troops - El Alamein
Allied countries
German controlled territory 1942
Extent of Japanese Empire 1942
Neutral countries
U-boat activity

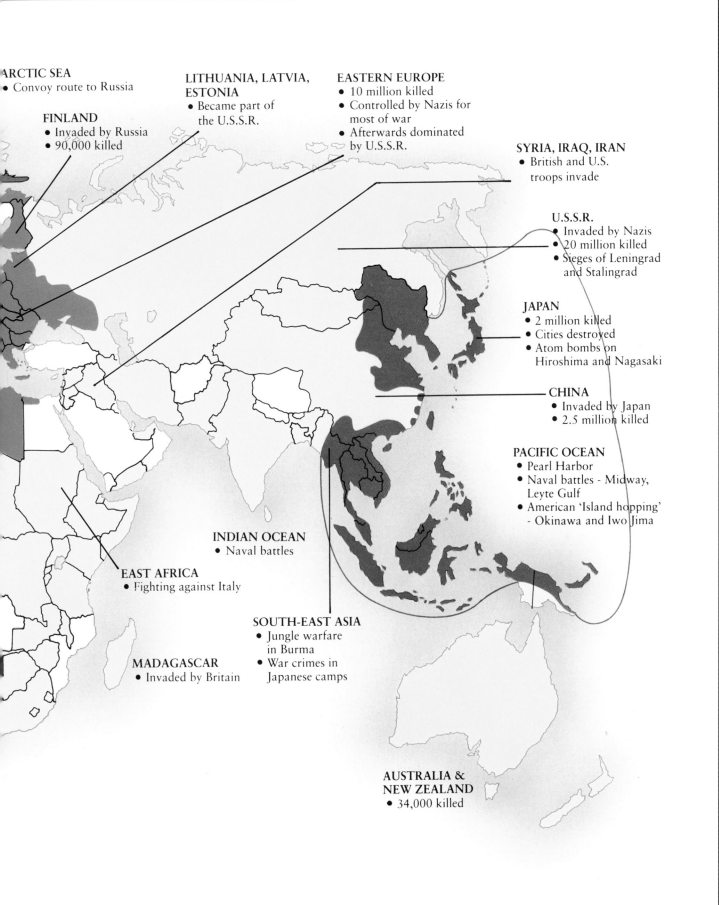

ARCTIC SEA
- Convoy route to Russia

FINLAND
- Invaded by Russia
- 90,000 killed

LITHUANIA, LATVIA, ESTONIA
- Became part of the U.S.S.R.

EASTERN EUROPE
- 10 million killed
- Controlled by Nazis for most of war
- Afterwards dominated by U.S.S.R.

SYRIA, IRAQ, IRAN
- British and U.S. troops invade

U.S.S.R.
- Invaded by Nazis
- 20 million killed
- Sieges of Leningrad and Stalingrad

JAPAN
- 2 million killed
- Cities destroyed
- Atom bombs on Hiroshima and Nagasaki

CHINA
- Invaded by Japan
- 2.5 million killed

PACIFIC OCEAN
- Pearl Harbor
- Naval battles - Midway, Leyte Gulf
- American 'Island hopping' - Okinawa and Iwo Jima

INDIAN OCEAN
- Naval battles

EAST AFRICA
- Fighting against Italy

SOUTH-EAST ASIA
- Jungle warfare in Burma
- War crimes in Japanese camps

MADAGASCAR
- Invaded by Britain

AUSTRALIA & NEW ZEALAND
- 34,000 killed

An End in Japan

IN THE FAR EAST, the Japanese armies achieved great advances in the early years of the war. They also committed terrible atrocities (war crimes). The Japanese Army's slogan was known as the 'three alls': 'Burn all, steal all, kill all'.

By 1945, however, Japan was on the edge of defeat. The American armies were slowly 'island-hopping' – advancing across the Pacific Ocean towards Japan, island by island.

They began to bomb mainland Japan. On 10 March 1945, American B29 bombers dropped a million firebombs on Tokyo, starting a fire which destroyed the city.

The Japanese threw everything into the war. Suicide kamikaze pilots flew their planes into American ships. Children were taken from the classrooms to work in the factories. In Japan, the Government said: 'Whatever may come, we are ready'.

◁ Young kamikaze pilots.

▽ High school girls are brought in to work at the ordnance factory.

▷ Devastation in Tokyo, 10 March 1945.

△ Japanese children often carried a younger brother or sister on their backs.

Sumiko Morikawa
Tokyo, 10 March 1945

When the American bombers attacked Tokyo, Sumiko Morikawa sheltered from the fire in a half-full swimming pool. Her two babies were strapped to her back, and she was holding her four-year-old son in her arms. This is the story of what became of the children:

"We went into the water, right beneath a burning school, and for several hours, until the school burned down, we had to endure a shower of sparks and embers. I could feel the babies on my back getting heavier and heavier. They were kicking me on both sides . . .

"Around the pool were heaps of bodies. You couldn't even tell if they were men or women. And the children – they were lying just like dummies all over the place. You could almost say you had to kick them out of the way to get through."

Sumiko got out of the pool and looked at the babies. "The two of them were just like dolls. Their faces were white, and they were dead. I put a little water in my son's mouth, and he was good enough to drink it for me, but that was really his last gasp. He said 'Mummy' to me in a very low voice, and then he just faded away.

"I thought I was doing all I could to protect them, but in the end I wasn't able to save any of them."

The Bomb

NOBODY could have been ready for the atom bombs which fell on Hiroshima and Nagasaki in August 1945.

The bomb on Hiroshima killed 71,000 people, and horribly injured another 100,000. Survivor Akira Ishida passed one woman, 'sitting on stone steps covered by blackened debris . . . Her entire body was charred and her hair was completely burned. She was embracing a red, burned baby in her arms and trying to breastfeed it with her red burned nipples, calling the baby's name again and again'. The Nagasaki bomb killed 40,000 more people.

Japan surrendered.

Even in America, some people asked whether the bomb should ever have been dropped. To Infantry-man Sheldon Johnson, however, waiting with the US Army to invade Japan, it seemed the right thing to do. 'I thought: "I feel bad that all those lives were lost", but it certainly saved mine . . . It saved many many lives. It was a beautiful, great thing.'

◁ The B29 bomber which dropped the atom bomb on Hiroshima.

▷ Devastation at Nagasaki.

▽ The atom bomb changed history. Nations continued testing atom bombs. They developed the more powerful Hydrogen bomb. Nothing was ever the same again.

WEL CO
HOM
HE CT

1945 – 1960

The End of the War

AFTER THE WAR, there were celebrations all over Europe. In Britain, people held street parties, waved flags and set off fireworks. For a moment, they forgot the horrors of the last five years.

Millions of soldiers went home to their families. Most were happy simply that the war had finished with an Allied victory. All were thankful to be alive.

It seemed as though the whole world was on the move. Millions of refugees were trudging across Europe – looking for loved ones, trying to get home, or fleeing westwards from the Russians. In Germany, Allied soldiers arrested Nazi officers, and forced ordinary Germans to go and visit the Nazi death camps.

◁ Russian and American soldiers at the end of the war.

▽ During the war, the Japanese had been told that the Americans would steal, kill and rape. They were surprised when their conquerors turned out to be friendly.

◁ VE Day in New York City. A couple embrace in the street.

▽ 'Daddy!' But many young children had never known what it was like to live with a man about the house. Some were quite frightened of their fathers.

Hard Times in Europe

AFTER THE WAR, American troops went home. People in the United States tried to get back to a life of 'cars, radios, vacuum cleaners, nylons [and] juicy steaks'.

But much of Europe lay in ruins. To make things worse, the winter of 1947 was one of the worst in living memory. 'After the war there was poverty and misery . . . there was nothing,' remembers Gerardo Ciola, who was living in the south of Italy.

How could Europe ever recover?

Help came from America. In the years after 1947, the Marshall Plan pumped $13 billion-worth of aid into 16 countries. Marshall Aid helped to restart Europe's coal mines and steel mills.

The Americans said they wanted to 'bind up the wounds of war'. They were shocked to find that many Europeans were suspicious of them, and thought it was a plot to take over Europe.

◁ A week's ration for two in Britain.

▽ Food shortages meant queuing for groceries.

△ A French farming family shows off the new tractor provided by Marshall Aid.

Evelyne Langey
Post-war France

Evelyne Langey was an orphan when France was liberated (freed) at the end of the war.

"I'd queue up for four or five hours with my jug and I'd come back with millet-seed – you feed it to birds now. The worst moment for me was when I was so hungry that for the only time in my life I wanted to steal a piece of steak from a butcher's stall. I must have passed that stall four times, but I could never pluck up the courage to do it, so I stayed hungry. But when you start having thoughts like that, it just goes to show how desperate the shortages were."

▷ Rebuilding Dresden after the war.

The Iron Curtain

BRITAIN, RUSSIA AND AMERICA had fought together to defeat Germany but they never really trusted each other.

After the war, distrust hardened into hatred.

Twenty million Russians had died in the war. The survivors were determined that Russia would never be invaded again. After Soviet occupation, all the countries in Eastern Europe fell under Communist control.

In March 1946, the British Prime Minister, Winston Churchill, visited the USA. He warned the

Americans of the growing Soviet power. Between Eastern and Western Europe, he told them, the Russians had built an 'Iron Curtain'. If, he warned, the democracies did not stand firm, Stalin's tyranny might spread further.

After the war, the Allies had divided Berlin into two. East Berlin was controlled by the Russians. West Berlin – deep inside Soviet-controlled Eastern Europe – was administered by the United States, Britain and France. In 1948, the Russians decided that they could take over West Berlin by starving the Berliners into submission. They cut off all communications and supply lines to West Berlin.

The Allies decided that West Berlin could not fall. For almost a year, they supplied all Berlin's needs by air. As a warning, in July 1948, B29 bombers (like the planes that had dropped the atom bomb on Hiroshima) were sent to bases in England.

In May 1949, the Soviets lifted the blockade. West Berlin would stay free.

In 1961, the Communists put up a wall to divide West Berlin from East Berlin – millions were escaping to the West through West Berlin. It was a visible symbol of Churchill's 'Iron Curtain'. To the West, it was 'a wall of shame'; to the Russians it was the 'anti-Fascist protective rampart'.

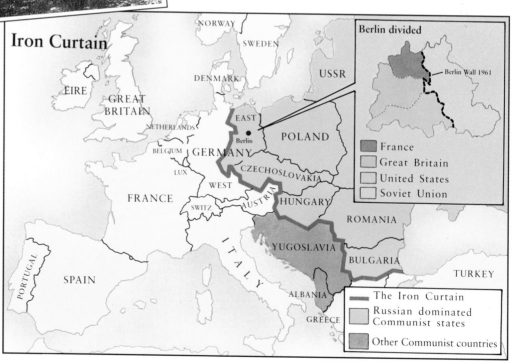

Iron Curtain

Berlin divided

Berlin Wall 1961

France
Great Britain
United States
Soviet Union

The Iron Curtain
Russian dominated Communist states
Other Communist countries

Mercedes Wild

West Berlin, 1948

During the Berlin airlift, Gail Halverson, an American airman, decided to drop chocolate on tiny parachutes to West Berlin children. Mercedes Wild wrote to him.

"'Dear Chocolate Uncle . . . Please throw a parachute into the Hennel Strasse, you will recognise the garden because of the white hen.' So I did that and I waited and waited . . . afterwards there was a letter, a small parcel. And there were chewing gums, a small piece of chocolate, a letter . . . I kept this letter. For me the letter was the answer from the Chocolate Uncle."

▽ Mercedes' drawing of the handkerchief parachutes.

▽ The US Air Force and the RAF flew 27,000 flights carrying 1.5 million tons of supplies into West Berlin. The airlift cost £100 million. To the pilots flying the the planes, the Berlin crisis seemed like a 'comparison of good and evil'.

Stalin's Russia

'GREAT LEADER for all eternity . . . you bring happiness to the world', sang the choir as the Krakow Philharmonic Orchestra performed the Stalin Cantata.

The 'great leader' of Soviet Russia was Josef Stalin. He encouraged a cult of personality which presented him as the hero of the Russian people. Photographs and history books were changed to make it seem that Stalin had taken a leading role in events. The Russians were told that their lifestyle was the envy of the world, and that Stalin had made it all possible.

At Stalin's 70th birthday celebrations in 1949, a little girl named Tamara Banketik gave him some flowers. Her speech summed up everything Stalin wanted to hear:

'We are children of Lenin and Stalin . . . Teacher, leader, beloved friend. Father Stalin, welcome!'

But Stalin's Russia was a sham; after the ceremony, she had to give back the dress she had worn.

Tamara Banketik
Minsk, 1949

Tamara Banketik was chosen to go to Moscow for the celebrations. It was a great contrast with her life of terrible poverty where 'I would sell cold water, and I had enough money to buy just a tiny piece of bread.'

"So, we came to Moscow . . . We had never seen such luxury . . . white beds, with bed sheets . . . After that we were taken to a restaurant and I felt very embarrassed because I didn't know how to use forks . . ."

◁ Statue of Stalin and Lenin: many Russians genuinely loved their leader, but there was real fear as well as love. For instance, the first person to stop clapping when the name of Stalin was mentioned tended to be arrested by the secret police!

▷ Stalin was paranoid in his suspicions. His secret police ran a regime of terror. Millions of Russians were sent to prison camps; thousands were executed.

▽ This propaganda painting shows Stalin with happy workers and peasants at the Dneiprostoi dam. Soviet citizens were never shown pictures of starving peasants or imprisoned Communists.

The Cold War

ACCORDING TO ONE AMERICAN NEWSREEL, all Communists were 'lying, dirty, shrewd, godless, murderous, determined . . . to destroy our Government'.

In the USSR, the Communists hated and feared the West as much as the West hated and feared the Communists. 'Show Trials' of 'traitors' were held. They encouraged loyal Russians to hate the Americans – and stopped dissatisfied Russians from opposing their Government.

After an American Senator called Joseph McCarthy had claimed that there were Communists all over the United States, the Americans also held public trials of 'traitors'. Hundreds of innocent, loyal Americans lost their jobs, their homes and their friends.

The two superpowers were not at war, but they were continually in conflict – it was the 'cold war'.

△ War broke out in Korea in 1950 when the United States fought the spread of Communism from North to South Korea.

◁ The Americans produced an imaginary propaganda film set in the town of Mosinee. The people pretended that they had been conquered by the Russians.

◁ Senator McCarthy

▷ In 1956 Hungarians tried without success to gain freedom from their Communist rulers.

The Atomic Age

WHY DIDN'T the 'cold war' between the superpowers develop into a Third World War between them?

The answer is: the atom bomb. Stalin's Russia got the atom bomb in September 1949. Soon, both superpowers had the more powerful Hydrogen bomb. Other countries developed atom bombs – Britain, France, China, India. By the 1960s, there were enough nuclear weapons to destroy every living thing on Earth many times over – 'overkill'.

◁ Troops were told to stand up and march towards the mushroom cloud. Afterwards they were dusted off with a broom; it was the only protection they got.

In the past, war had always been a last resort: the way to destroy your enemy. But if your enemy had the atom bomb, war was simply a way to destroy yourself. To go to war was to commit national suicide. It was MAD: 'mutually assured destruction'.

Also, in the past, politicians had sent other people to die for their schemes if it came to war. Now, they were going to be asked to die for their own schemes.

So the atom bomb changed the way countries conducted their diplomacy! The superpowers threatened war. They postured and blustered. But they always pulled back from the brink.

▽ In America, scientists worked frantically to keep ahead of the Soviets. Little care was taken of the population; tests were made only 75 miles from Las Vegas. 60,000 troops took part in the experiments.

Alexei Kosmich Kondratiev
Russia, 1946

Stalin demanded the atom bomb, whatever the cost. He put Beria, his chief of police in charge of the project. At only fifteen, the young Kondratiev was a lab assistant in charge of workers at the research centre.

"It is hard for me to judge about the race. After all, I was only fifteen . . . We were afraid of you, you were probably afraid of us, it's no longer a secret. We worked day and night . . . I was left to start up the reactor for Beria to see."

Ban the Bomb

WHAT WOULD YOU DO if there was a nuclear attack?

The British Government developed a complicated system of warnings – either by siren or church bells. In Scotland, where they had neither sirens nor church bells, it hoped to rely on 'word of mouth or whistle'. Then people were told to rush and shelter under their kitchen tables. This was supposed to happen in the four minutes they had before Russian nuclear missiles hit Britain!

It was clearly ridiculous. In fact, everyone expected to die if there was a nuclear war. People lived in fear of Armageddon – the end of the world.

In the past, people had tended to trust the 'experts'. But as the results of nuclear war and the dangers of nuclear testing became clear, more and more people came to believe that 'when politicians fail, people must give the lead'. The atom bomb changed the way that the people treated their leaders. The present-day suspicion that all politicians are stupid and self-seeking had its roots in the Ban the Bomb marches, when, for the first time, ordinary people stood up and said that they knew better than their betters.

▽ The United States Government gave American schoolchildren some survival tips in a newsreel called 'Duck and Cover'. Good boys and girls, 'no matter where they go or what they do, they always try to remember what to do if the atom bomb explodes right then.' 'It's a bomb! Duck and cover!'

All this would have been utterly useless if an atom bomb had actually exploded. The measures were simply to reassure the public that the Government knew what it was doing, and to increase people's fear and hatred of 'the enemy'.

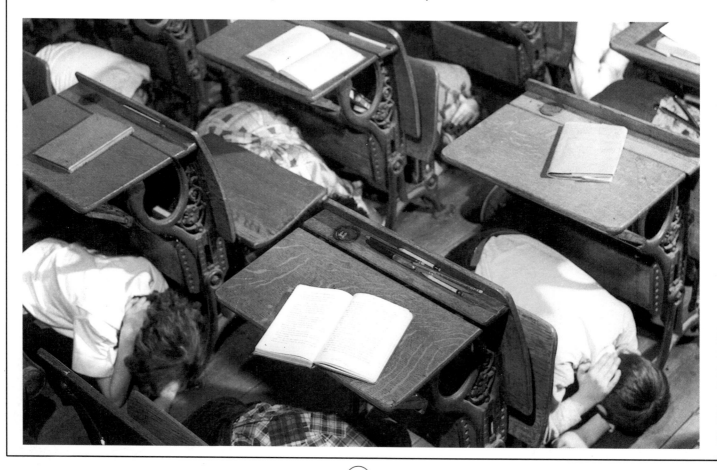

▷ Cuban propaganda poster. In 1962 the US nuclear strike force prepared for war against Russia when it was proved that the Russians were building missile sites in Castro's Cuba. The crisis – and nuclear war – was averted when Khrushchev agreed with Kennedy that the missiles should be removed.

▽ 'Ban the Bomb' marchers.

Freedom Now

DURING THE SECOND World War, the Allies motivated their soldiers by telling them that they were fighting for freedom and the right to choose their own Government.

Yet for centuries, the countries of Europe had had huge overseas empires. They controlled a fifth of the world's land surface. They reassured themselves that foreign rule was good for the colonies. 'Say "Well done!" to the social works; they have raised the level of education, of health and of happiness of the inhabitants,' claimed a French newsreel. But actually, the real purpose of empire was profit, not charity.

After the Second World War, India was the first British colony to gain independence, in 1947.

Birenda Kaur
India, 1947

Birenda Kaur was a schoolgirl when India gained independence.

"When the dawn came – I cannot describe to you how heady the feeling was. It was as though everything was new. The world was new. The trees were greener . . . . It was too fantastic. You felt you could do anything, now that we were free."

△ Indian Independence, August 1947.

◁ The Indian movement for independence was led by Mahatma Gandhi. He organised a peaceful campaign of strikes and boycotts.

▷ The creation of India and Pakistan led to 30 million people becoming refugees – Muslims fleeing to Pakistan, and Hindus fleeing to India. Hundreds of thousands were killed in violent fighting between Muslims and Hindus.

Partition of India

Kashmir (disputed)

AFGHANISTAN

WEST PAKISTAN

Karachi

CHINA

BHUTAN

NEPAL

INDIA

Dacca

Calcutta

Bombay

BURMA

EAST PAKISTAN (Bangladesh since 1971)

CEYLON (Sri Lanka since 1972)

△ The British 'Raj' (empire) in India was partitioned into three independent countries: India, Pakistan and Burma.

A Wind of Change

INDIA'S LEADER GANDHI said: 'If India can break free, others will follow.'

'A wind of change' was blowing in Africa also. Ghana was the first African country to be given independence, in 1957. Others quickly followed. In Africa there was a mood of joy and hope. Kwame Nkrumah, the new leader of Ghana, told the All African Peoples' Conference: 'Forward then to independence. Tomorrow: the United States of Africa'.

△ Kwame Nkrumah, leader of Ghana.

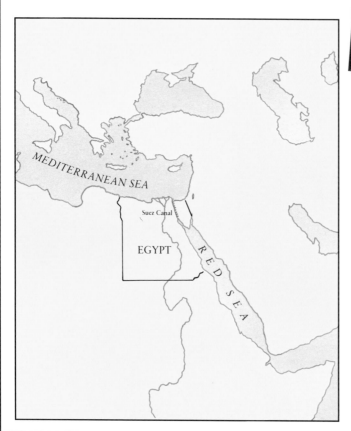

However, independence was the beginning, not the end, of Africa's problems. Borders drawn by Europeans, which ignored old tribal boundaries, led to civil wars within the new African states. The new countries did not have enough Government officials. They found it hard to achieve economic growth. Many of them quickly fell prey to corrupt military dictators. Although the African nations gained freedom from the old empires, few had freedom from hunger, disease, poverty or oppression.

◁ In 1956, Britain and France tried to take control of the Suez Canal from Egypt. In a humiliating climbdown, they were forced to withdraw their troops. Many African countries realised that European supremacy in Africa was ended.

Anim Assiful
Ghana, 1957

Anim Assiful used to help his father, who was a cocoa planter in Ghana. He believed the British Government fixed prices in order to protect British interests.

"There were a lot of British companies in the cocoa business. They sent their agents out to buy cocoa from the villages. We didn't have our own scales for weighing the beans, so we were really cheated by the agents. We had to accept the prices they gave us. The price was set by the British and we had no say. Our hands were tied."

◁ In British-controlled Kenya, the colonists had settled vast areas of land. The African Kikuyu people said that the land belonged to them. A guerrilla organisation called the Mau Mau waged a terror campaign against the whites, attacking isolated farms and settlers. In these homes children were accustomed to the presence of a loaded rifle. Although the British were ruthless with the Mau Mau, they were still forced to give Kenya independence in 1963.

▷ When the Belgian Congo became independent, the European colonists – who had believed that the black Africans should be ruled with harsh discipline – left. With them went most of the administrative and industrial expertise. The Congo dissolved into chaos and civil war.

Japan's Economic Miracle

JAPAN'S MINISTRY of Munitions had run Japanese industry during the Second World War. It continued to do so after the war, although it was now called the Ministry of International Trade and Industry (MITI). It had the same officials. It used the same methods. It organised raw materials. It arranged loans. It paid for research. Out of sight of Western businessmen, Japan developed the best system of management in the world.

The Japanese economy grew quickly. By 1969, Japan had overtaken Britain, France and West Germany. Between 1960 and 1968 the average income of Japanese workers doubled.

By the 1970s, Western businessmen were going to Japan to learn how to run their companies better.

▽ By the mid 1970s, many of Japan's products are better quality and more reliable than those of the West.

▷ Japan's education system stresses discipline, obedience and hard work.

▷ An exercise class for factory workers in Tokyo.

Thirty Glorious Years

'AFTER THE WAR we had what we call the 30 glorious years. The life was very easy. We had good jobs. We had money to spend and it seemed that all our dreams came true.'

That is how Monette Gaunt remembers life in France in the 1950s and 60s – a life of consumer durables: washing machines, refrigerators, dishwashers, cookers, television and – most of all – motor cars.

After the Second World War, such affluence was to be found only in America. This wealth was based on mass-production and cheap credit (buying on 'the never-never'). The American worker earned more than any worker in history, yet still had leisure time each day to enjoy life.

The affluence quickly spread to Europe. In 1959, Harold Macmillan, the British Prime Minister, told the British people: 'You've never had it so good'. And he was right.

It seemed that the good times could go on for ever.

Consumer durables – scooters, washing machine, radio. Did they really allow women freedom, or did they trap them into a 'little housewife' way of life?

▽ The American way: Coca-Cola and a Cadillac.

Picture Post, 7 August, 1954. Registered at the G.P.O. as a Newspaper.

Come on – let's have a 'COKE'!

Coca-Cola is real refreshment for everybody—
any time of day. Out and about, or at home
with the family, it's always the right time
and place for 'Coke'. Pure and wholesome,
delicious and refreshing, Coca-Cola is unlike
any other drink in the world. Enjoy 'Coke'
whenever you feel like a 'break'—and return
to work (or play) wonderfully refreshed!

Drink
Coca-Cola
TRADE MARK REG.

'Coca-Cola' and 'Coke' are the regd.
trade marks of The Coca-Cola Co.

Call it 'Coke' or ... the same delicious drink

Caryn Pace
United States, 1950s

Caryn Pace grew up in Long Island, near New York, in the 1950s.

"My mom was a housewife and a mother and she stayed home, and my father was a roofer, so he was a blue collar worker ... I was his pride and joy, needless to say – Daddy's little girl – and he couldn't do enough for me, and neither could my mother. They were brought up through the Depression and the war. Obviously I was part of the baby boomers after the war, and they just wanted to see me have what they couldn't.

"There were a few Christmases that were really great. I had five or six dolls, maybe four stuffed animals, three games, two educational toys and a set of drums, so we had a lot of fun with that. My mother could have given up the drum set.

"It was golden. I got everything I wanted. I couldn't have asked for anything more as a child."

1960–2000

The Death of a Dream

ON 22 NOVEMBER 1963, the American President, John F. Kennedy, was assassinated.

Since the Second World War, the Western world had prospered. People were full of hope and confidence. Kennedy was young and handsome. He was a symbol of people's belief that humankind was on its way to a better, new life.

So Kennedy's death shocked and saddened them. Many people alive at the time can remember exactly what they were doing when they heard the news. It was not just that a nice young man had been killed. His death made them aware that their hopes had just been a dream.

People realised that the world was not a happy place which would automatically get better and better. It was a world of heartbreak and oppression. And it was these – the 'issues for a modern world' – that people had to face.

This chapter looks at how they tackled those issues.

△ What made Kennedy's death so dramatic was that millions of people around the world could follow the events on television.

▽ Death on film – the assassination as filmed by Orville Nix. Picture 2 shows the moment when the President was shot.

1

2

3

▷ Kennedy's funeral. By this time Lee Harvey Oswald, the man charged with Kennedy's murder, was also dead – shot on live TV. The quiet dignity of Jacqueline Kennedy, and the picture of Kennedy's son John saluting his father's coffin, moved to tears many of the people who watched the funeral on television.

④

⑤

⑥

Civil Rights

HOW IMPORTANT is the colour of a person's skin? It used to matter a lot in the United States. The US Constitution declared that all people were equal. But local laws – especially in the southern states – often discriminated against blacks. Blacks were not allowed to sit in the front seats on buses. They were not allowed to go to school with white children. They could not eat in white restaurants. In some places, although blacks were entitled to vote in the United States, there were still white officials who refused to register them as voters.

In the 1960s, American blacks began to demand their 'civil rights'.

△ In 1965, Martin Luther King led 25,000 people on a march from Selma to Montgomery in Alabama. Months later, the Voting Rights Act was signed into law.

◁ In the 1960s, black and white Civil Rights protesters went and sat together in white restaurants. They were trained to remain calm even when attacked. In 1964, the Civil Rights Law prohibited racial discrimination in restaurants and other public places.

Ernest Green
Little Rock, United States, 1957

In 1954 the American Supreme Court ruled that black and white children should be educated in the same schools. But when nine black children tried to go to Little Rock High School, in 1957, the local Governor sent soldiers to keep them out. In reply, the US Government sent in Federal troops, who escorted the children into school past a mob of 1,000 white protesters:

"We were in a station wagon. In the front was an army jeep with a machine gun mount, and behind us was another army jeep ... A cordon of soldiers surrounded us ...

"It really was an exhilarating feeling that you had finally accomplished something. You could see the cameras and the people across the street and that all of it was focused on the nine of us going to the school."

▽ Teenagers being escorted into Little Rock High School by Federal troops.

The 'Great Leap'

IN OCTOBER 1949, the Communist revolutionaries took power in China.

The leader of China's new Communist Government was Mao Tse Tung. Mao wanted China to become a world power. In 1958, he asked the Chinese people to make a 'Great Leap Forward'. The peasants were herded into huge communes. They ate food cooked in central kitchens. Children were looked after together. Mao announced that food production had to double in a year. Communes competed to produce the highest yields. But the experiment was a disaster. Crops rotted in the fields because the peasants, wanting to increase the yield per acre, put the plants too close together.

The result was a famine which killed over 20 million people.

The Great Leap failed. Mao lost some of his influence.

Then, in 1966, Mao took back power. He said that he wanted a 'Cultural Revolution'. He appealed to China's young people. They became his 'Red Guards'. He told them to attack the 'four olds' – old habits, old ideas, old customs and old culture.

The Cultural Revolution was also a disaster. In the end, the Red Guards started to attack each other. After two years, the movement was completely out of control. The Army had to be called in to restore order, and the young people were sent to the countryside to 'cool off'. Mao Tse Tung died in 1976.

▽ Children in the Red Guards play war games. Here a boy with a wooden rifle attacks the opponents of the Revolution (in white capes).

The Cultural Revolution. Eleven million students and children came to a succession of huge rallies in Tianamen Square in Beijing. They all carried a 'Little Red Book' containing Mao Tse Tung's ideas. They were fanatical in their obedience to Chairman Mao.

Shao Ai Ling

China, 1960s

During the Cultural Revolution, young people were encouraged to rebel against the authorities, and to attack Mao's rivals. They attacked foreign ambassadors, local officials and businessmen – even their teachers. Shao Ai Ling was a headmistress in Shanghai:

"There were several hundred Red Guards wearing arm bands, others had military belts. Some had scissors in their hands, ready to cut people's hair. They chopped off my hair and beat me with sticks ... They said: 'How dare you say you love Chairman Mao. You deserve to be overthrown ...'

"It was December in Shanghai and very cold. They ordered me to stand outside in the playground from morning to night. But then they thought the punishment wasn't severe enough. So they got a big blackboard and pressed it down on me. One of them stood on the right side, and one on the left like a see-saw, and I was squashed in the middle."

Health for All

THE SECOND World War was fought against a human enemy. After the war, governments began the fight against humankind's real enemies – poverty, homelessness and disease.

Western governments set up systems of public health, such as the British National Health Service. People were given medical care, clean water and good sewers as a right.

At the same time, medical miracles defeated disease. Wonder drugs such as penicillin cured a whole range of illnesses. Brilliant surgeons learned how to replace even the human heart.

In 1948 the World Health Organisation was set up by the United Nations. Its aim is 'Health for all' by the year 2000.

▽ Manila, Philippines, where nearly half of all families live below the poverty level.

▷ Before the Second World War, 2.5 million people died yearly from smallpox. The WHO waged a war against smallpox. Millions were vaccinated. The bacteria is now extinct.

Deborah Runkle
United States, 1954

Nowadays, we have come to expect that doctors will make us better when we are ill. We find it hard to understand how excited people got when they were given the chance to escape from illness.

In 1953 the American doctor Jonas Salk discovered a vaccine against polio.

Deborah Runkle was one of the first children to be given the vaccine:

"My father called our doctor. He didn't have enough for all his patients: he just had some. My father said: 'Make it be my children. My three children. See that my children get it . . .'

"And we went and got the vaccine. And then it was over. That was the fix. There was no more polio. There was no more worry."

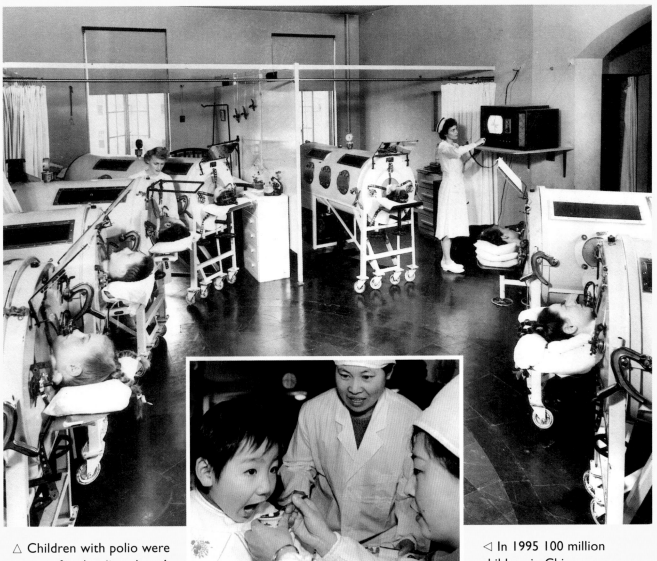

△ Children with polio were confined to 'iron lungs'.

◁ In 1995 100 million children in China were immunised against polio.

Vietnam

THE COMMUNISTS of Vietnam (the 'Vietcong') had used guerrilla methods of warfare to drive the French out of south-east Asia in 1954. When a non-Communist state was set up in South Vietnam, the Vietcong vowed to destroy it the same way.

The United States tried to help the South Vietnam Government. In the end, 600,000 American troops were fighting in Vietnam.

The Americans fought a conventional war. They bombed supply lines. They sent troops on 'search and destroy missions' to find and kill the enemy.

But where was the enemy? They moved unseen through the forests. They ambushed the Americans

▷ The Vietcong used a maze of underground tunnels to fight the Americans.

▽ The Americans bombed the forests with Agent Orange (a chemical which stripped the leaves from trees) and napalm (a sticky, petrol-based gel, which burned the victim). The little girl had her clothes burned away with napalm. She now lives in the United States.

Tran Thi Gung

Vietnam, 1960s

For the Vietcong, the Vietnam war was a 'People's War'. The whole population had to drive out the Americans. Teenagers became hardened killers. Tran Thi Gung joined the Vietcong when her father was killed.

"I gained the titles two times because I had killed a lot of Americans ... about 10 ...When we were in the tunnels we couldn't eat or go to the toilet because it was very difficult. We just ate fried rice and drank very little water. After seven or eight days we could make the hole up to the surface of the ground and the air would follow that hole to come into the tunnels."

and ran away, or left land mines and booby traps for them. One American unit was known as the 'Hard Luck Battalion'. In six months it suffered 600 casualties dead or wounded, but never saw an enemy soldier. The Vietcong mingled with the ordinary people. It seemed as though the whole population was the enemy.

American and South Vietnamese soldiers burned villages to the ground. They killed and tortured the enemy soldiers they captured. A million Vietnamese civilians were killed in the fighting. By the end of the war, many ordinary Vietnamese did support the Vietcong.

In 1968 the Vietcong launched a massive offensive. It was eventually defeated. But it convinced many Americans that they would never win. Protesters in the United States called for the end of the war.

In 1973, the Americans pulled out. The Vietcong had defeated the greatest military power on earth.

US Marines and helicopters in Vietnam.

Yippee!

MORE CHILDREN were born in the ten years after the Second World War than in the half century before. By 1960, they were teenagers. Half the population was under 18, and a new youth culture set the tone of life in the Western world.

Young people had the time and the money to enjoy themselves. At the same time, there was a feeling that the world was about to end in a nuclear war. Penny Hayes was a schoolgirl in England:

'I can remember coming home from school one day and saying to my mother, "Don't you realise I've got to live now because we're going to kill ourselves soon. Someone's going to drop the bomb."'

The new youth culture started with Rock'n'Roll music. If parents hated it, all the better.

In California, many young people became 'hippies'. They 'dropped out' and sought an 'alternative culture' based on peace and love – and, also, drugs and sex.

Many young people wanted to make the world a better place. They joined the Civil Rights movement, or the Ban the Bomb marches. All over the world there were demonstrations against the Vietnam War. When the marches were attacked by the police, protests turned to violence. In 1968 there were riots in France, Japan and America. In America the 'Yippies' also threatened to put the drug LSD into the water supply, and nominated a pig for President. Their leader Abbie Hoffman declared: 'We are the second American Revolution. We are winning: Yippee!'

△ For most young people, 'rebelling' was nothing more than wearing 'way out' clothes and growing their hair long.

◁ The pop group The Beatles were greeted with such frenzy that adults thought the young people had gone mad: it was called 'Beatlemania'.

△ Paris, France, 1968. University students from the Sorbonne are attacked by riot police.

◁ The Vietnam War became a focus of student anger. This American protester burns the draft card calling him up for the army.

The Power of Youth

△ Elvis Presley in the 1960s

THERE WAS NO world-wide youth revolution in the 1960s. Most young people did not want violent change. Others were put off by the deaths of pop idols like Jimi Hendrix, Jim Morrison and Janis Joplin. The youth revolution of the 1960s 'burned out'.

But young people continued to gain ever greater influence and freedom. Shops started to sell the things they wanted. Teachers were forbidden to hit children. In Sweden, it is against the law for parents to smack their children. In America, a child divorced his parents.

Pop music and fashions have continued to change rapidly, but they are increasingly 'just for fun' and personal satisfaction. And although many young people still care about the things that are wrong with the world, there is no longer a naive call to destroy 'the system'. Nowadays, young people get involved in the so-called 'single issues' such as Animal Rights or the Environment, and lobby 'the system' to change.

Pop stars, particularly those from Britain and America, have set the pace for youth culture and fashion throughout the second half of the century.

△ Jimi Hendrix, c. 1968

◁ The Beatles in 1966

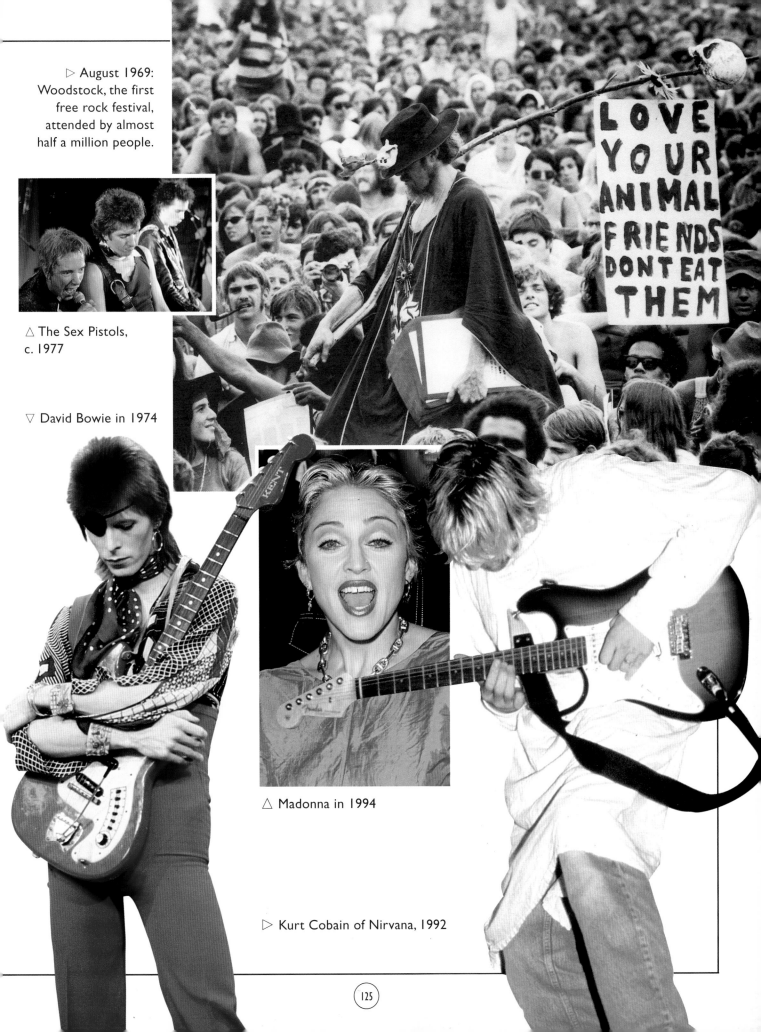

▷ August 1969: Woodstock, the first free rock festival, attended by almost half a million people.

△ The Sex Pistols, c. 1977

▽ David Bowie in 1974

LOVE YOUR ANIMAL FRIENDS DONT EAT THEM

△ Madonna in 1994

▷ Kurt Cobain of Nirvana, 1992

Out of the Kitchen

DURING THE Second World War, many Western women had key jobs in industry. After the war, they were expected to go back to being housewives.

Most of those who did work were stuck in unskilled, low-paid, 'dead end' jobs. In 1963, an American housewife called Betty Friedan wrote *The Feminine Mystique*. It criticised 'the dull routine of housework'. Many women who read it realised that they were just as good as the men. They campaigned for equal opportunities. Since children were the main tie on a woman's life, the 'feminists' also campaigned for birth control and abortion.

The United Nations declared 1975 'the International Year of the Woman'. They held a world conference in Mexico City. There, however, Betty Friedan clashed with women from the Third World, who were more bothered about clean water, housing and food than about promotion prospects.

△ The first need of women in Third World countries is for a decent standard of living.

◁ The feminists wanted women to come out of the kitchen – the American *Life* magazine listed a woman's weekly chores as: 35 beds to make, 750 items to wash up, 400 pieces of silverware to polish, 80 kilos of food to cook and 250 pieces of laundry to wash and iron.

One of the problems facing women in employment is that too often they are expected to do this *as well as* their full-time jobs.

Dusty Roads
United States, 1950s

When Dusty Roads became an air stewardess, the airline companies rejected applicants who were awkward, less than friendly, bit their nails, wore glasses, were married or over 32 years of age. She campaigned against this discrimination. Here she talks about the career prospects for an American girl in the 1950s, and the changes that have happened since:

"It was really very limited to rather *boring* things. You could be a nurse, a librarian or a schoolteacher. And these things I just checked off as being: '*boring*!' . . .

"I could be a doctor instead of a nurse, be a pilot now instead of a flight attendant, be a Senator instead of a secretary . . .

"It gives me a big thrill when I go up to that cockpit and I see a girl there and I know that I have something to do with it."

Mercedes Sanchez
Mexico

At the start of the century, a woman in the Third World could expect to have 12 children, and to live only to the age of 40. Mercedes Sanchez campaigned in Mexico City to get human living standards for her family.

"From the time I was seven I worked. If you didn't work you didn't have anything to eat . . . They would give me something to stand on so I could reach the sink. That's been my life, washing clothes . . .

"I had twelve children. Of the twelve, five lived, the rest I lost. That's it exactly. I lost them because I didn't have what they needed when they were sick. The loss of my children hurts me . . . That's how we began the fight, for a dignified living situation for our children."

▽ New York, early 1970s. Thousands of women march for equality with men.

Endangered Planet

IN THE YEARS AFTER after the Second World War, industrialists had expanded production without a thought for the environment. Factories belched out smoke and fumes. Cars 'guzzled' petrol. People accepted waste and dust as something that went with progress.

'We accepted it as a part of life … the stench, the smoke, the absolute filth that filled our lungs and made some of us ill. But we thought this was the way life was – the way God intended …'

But as time went on, people realised that the destruction of nature had to stop. They began to force their governments to make laws to protect the environment. Today, people realise that pollution is a global issue of life and death:

'Without protecting the environment we cannot survive. Even if profits have to suffer, the environment must come first.'

▷ The first moon walk, in 1969, helped to change the way people thought about pollution. Looking back from the moon, the Earth seemed very small and fragile. People realised that this was the only Earth we'd got. They realised that pollution was not just a local problem, but a world issue.

Lois Gibbs
Love Canal, United States, 1970s

The American suburb of Love Canal was built on top of ground that had been used in the 1940s as a waste dump for 20,000 tons of toxic waste. In the 1970s, the drums began to leak. Lois Gibbs and local protesters locked officials into a building until they agreed to re-house the residents.

"When we first moved to Love Canal my son Michael, who was just one year old, was perfectly healthy . . .

"In the next four years Michael developed epilepsy, a liver disease, a urinary tract disorder, which required two surgeries to correct. He developed severe asthma. And this is just a five-year-old child."

▽ Love Canal

▽ The first environmental issue: in the 1950s, the Chisso chemical factory at Minemata in Japan simply poured its waste into the bay where local fishermen fished. Local people developed symptoms of mercury poisoning – paralysis and shaking fits. Babies were born paralysed or brain-damaged. The damage to the environment was permanent. It is still not possible to fish in Minemata Bay.

◁ Victims of radioactive poisoning from the Chernobyl nuclear reactor explosion in 1986.

Afghanistan

Unnamed Afghan child
Afghanistan, 1986

It is possible for a motivated rebel army to win a guerrilla war, but the cost to the ordinary people is terrible. This eight-year-old boy wept as he described what happened when the Russians came to his village:

"They shot my father with three bullets: in his chest, his shoulder, and the back of his neck. He fell down dead. My brother and his friend the commander got very angry and fought with them. My brother jumped and grabbed one of their weapons.

"At this point, more Russians came, and my brother's fingers were cut off by a bayonet ... so of course he was helpless. After all his fingers had been cut off, they beat him. They shot him in one ear, and the bullet came out of the other."

A COMMUNIST GOVERNMENT had taken power in Afghanistan in the 1970s. When it came under attack from Muslim rebels in 1979, the Soviet Union sent 100,000 troops to defend it.

But it was impossible to wipe out the rebels. The Muslim guerrillas – called the Mujaheddin – hid in the mountains or mingled unnoticed among the ordinary people of Afghanistan.

The Mujaheddin believed that they were fighting a Holy War. They prayed five times a day. They kissed the Koran (the Muslim holy book) before they went into battle. They believed that they would go straight to paradise if they died fighting the Russians.

In 1989, the Russians withdrew. Soon after, the rebels captured Kabul, the capital city of Afghanistan. The Mujaheddin had won.

△ Rebels pray before a captured Russian tank.

◁ Young Muslim rebels with old guns and wooden sticks.

▷ The Mujaheddin rode on horseback to ambush Soviet supply columns. The guerrillas were merciless; 15,000 Russian troops were killed in 10 years.

God Fights Back

FOR MOST of the twentieth century, Western ideas and technology changed the world.

Even in Muslim countries such as Turkey and Egypt, rulers introduced Western ways. Women's lives changed dramatically. They stopped wearing the traditional Muslim veil. They were given the vote. They could go to university and get a job.

But in some areas of the Muslim countries, a different attitude grew up. To many, it seemed that Western 'freedom' was only the freedom to be greedy, sinful and dishonest. They were 'fundamentalists' – Muslims who wanted to return to the traditional Muslim ways.

In Iran, the Shah (king) wanted to 'Westernise' his country. But his Government was corrupt. He used

△ President Sadat. Financed by money from Iran, fundamentalist missionaries went to Egypt. They gave medicines and food to the poor; and they taught them that God is more important than governments. When President Sadat of Egypt came into conflict with Muslim fundamentalists, he was assassinated (in 1981).

△ Iraqi soldiers during the Iran-Iraq war

Said Sharifi Manesh
Iran, 1980

In 1980 Saddam Hussein, the ruler of Iraq, invaded Iran. The Iraqis were better equipped than the Iranian forces, and used poison gas. Thousands of Iranian children offered their lives to defend Islam.

It is difficult for people in the West to understand their commitment. Said Manesh was 13 years old when he joined up. He was wounded six times and returned home a war hero. But he regrets that he did not die, like his two elder brothers:

"They let me go to the war front and I really liked it. I was crying because I loved it so much. This was such pride that God had given me. It was a blessing from God . . .

"I was jealous that my brothers were killed. I felt that God had accepted them and not accepted me – that they were so good and so pure that God had taken them to Him. I felt that I was sinful and that God had not accepted me. I regretted that I had not become a martyr."

his SAVAK (secret police) to stay in power. In 1979, he was driven out. A Muslim fundamentalist leader – the Ayatollah Khomeini – took power.

Khomeini set up 'the Government of God' in Iran. A council of religious leaders was given the right to overturn the Parliament's decisions. Alcohol was banned. The Government brought back traditional Muslim punishments such as chopping off hands and stoning. Women were told to wear the veil and stay at home.

Fundamentalism is a growing influence in many Muslim countries. Even governments which do not want to return to traditional ways are having to change their policies, for fear of revolution.

△ Militant Muslims are prepared to commit acts of terrorism in support of their cause. In October 1983, a suicide bomber drove a truck into the American airport compound in Beirut, the capital city of the Lebanon. He was a devout Muslim from a poor Lebanese family. In the explosion, 241 Americans were killed.

▷ Tehran, 1979. A little girl wearing the traditional chador of Islamic women demonstrates in front of the US Embassy. She holds a picture of the Ayatollah Khomeini.

Revolutions against Revolution

BY 1985, after forty years of Communism, the governments of eastern Europe were in trouble. Factories were out-of-date, and there was no money to modernise them. They produced shoddy goods which were ugly and dangerous. Empty shops and food queues were a way of life.

Communist governments had little support from ordinary people. They kept power by censorship and the secret police. It was no use protesting. The system was backed by Soviet military power. When Polish workers went on strike in 1980, the Soviet Army assembled on the border with Poland. Soon after, the Polish Government crushed the strike.

Then, on 11 March 1985, Mikhail Gorbachev became the new General Secretary of the Communist Party of the Soviet Union. He admitted that the Soviet Union was having problems. He wanted perestroika (rebuilding). He encouraged glasnost (openness). For the first time in years, there was freedom of speech in the Soviet Union.

In 1989, the people of Poland forced their Communist leaders to hold an election. The Communists did not win a single seat. Poland became a free, Western-style country. The Government's limousines were used by new 'rent-a-limo' firms. The ideological training centre was turned into a nightclub.

◁ Lech Walesa, who was elected President of Poland in 1990.

▽ Mikhail Gorbachev

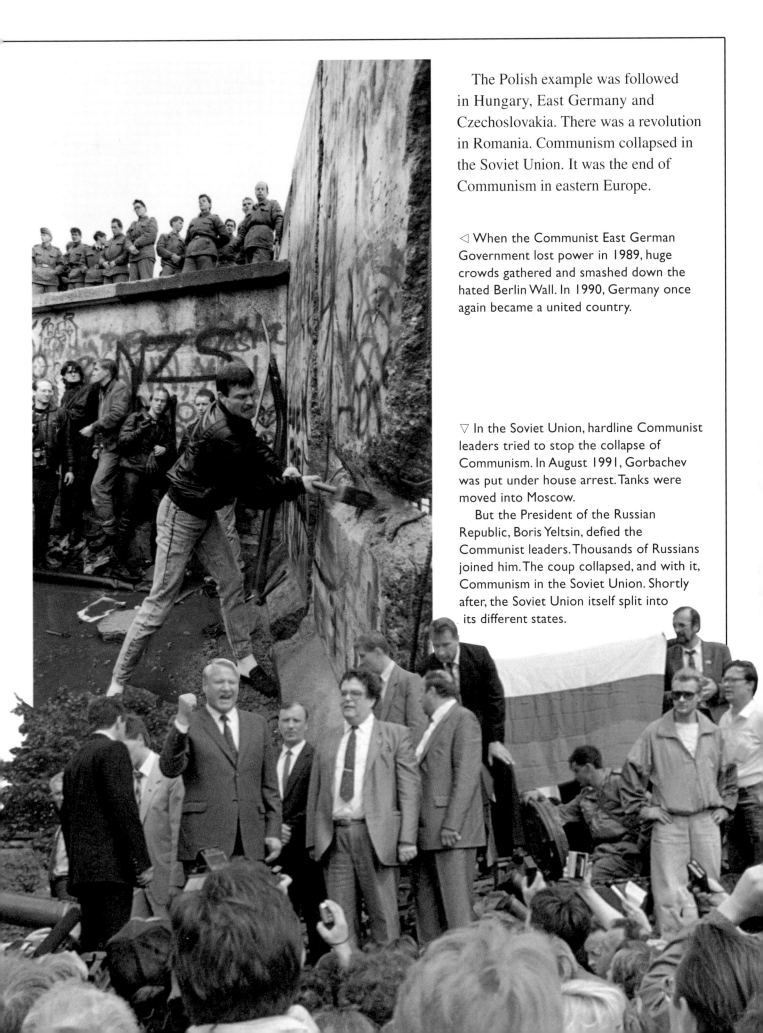

The Polish example was followed in Hungary, East Germany and Czechoslovakia. There was a revolution in Romania. Communism collapsed in the Soviet Union. It was the end of Communism in eastern Europe.

◁ When the Communist East German Government lost power in 1989, huge crowds gathered and smashed down the hated Berlin Wall. In 1990, Germany once again became a united country.

▽ In the Soviet Union, hardline Communist leaders tried to stop the collapse of Communism. In August 1991, Gorbachev was put under house arrest. Tanks were moved into Moscow.

But the President of the Russian Republic, Boris Yeltsin, defied the Communist leaders. Thousands of Russians joined him. The coup collapsed, and with it, Communism in the Soviet Union. Shortly after, the Soviet Union itself split into its different states.

Ali Zepta
Soweto, South Africa, 1976

Many black children from Soweto joined the guerrillas who were fighting against apartheid. At the age of 16, Ali Zepta ran away to train in Angola:

"I saw myself as a Jesus, who was coming to preach the word of liberation . . . I saw myself as Moses, who was going to lead them out of Egypt . . . This gun in my hand was my Bible – I was going to be the one that's going to prove that we can do it."

△ Riots in Cape Town in 1994.

▷ When black South Africans were finally given the vote in 1994, they queued for miles to cast their vote. It was so important to them. It was their victory over apartheid – 'a burial of something very evil'.

The End of Apartheid

IN 1948, the Government of South Africa made a decision to keep people of different races apart. Blacks were forced to move to the 'Bantustans' – their so-called tribal 'homelands'. All black people had to carry 'passbooks', with details of their race, employment and address. Any black caught without a passbook was arrested.

All protests were viciously put down. In 1960, at Sharpeville, a crowd of 20,000 people demonstrated against the passbook laws. The police opened fire on them; 69 demonstrators were killed.

People demanding one-man-one-vote were put on trial for treason. The black leader Nelson Mandela was sentenced to life imprisonment. The world turned against South Africa. Many countries boycotted South African products. As pressure grew, the South African Government was forced to abolish apartheid in 1994.

NON-EUROPEANS & GOODS

Nelson Mandela celebrates his election victory with F.W. de Klerk, the former President.

The Power of the Box

THE BBC STARTED regular television broadcasts in 1936. Nobody suspected that half a century later millions of people throughout the world would have television sets, which could receive dozens of channels, bringing live news coverage from all over the world.

Television has changed the world, as well as served it. Libraries, cinemas, churches, even football matches have suffered declining attendances. People's material wants have been affected by television advertising. Their political opinions are shaped by what they see 'on the box'.

△ In 1960, television affected politics. Presidential candidates John F. Kennedy and Richard Nixon held a public debate. Those who listened on radio thought that Nixon had won; those who watched the television thought that Kennedy had won. From that point onwards, politicians had to take care of their TV images.

▽ In 1968, Russian troops invaded Czechoslovakia. Czechoslovakian television commentators broadcast pictures of what was going on. They became part of the resistance to the Russians.

▽ Millions of people, all over the world, watched the moon walk, live, as it happened in 1969. It was the first live broadcast from space.

△ The first satellite – Telstar – was launched in 1962. It allowed a television link between Europe and the United States.

△ In the 1960s and 1970s, the American public watching reports from Vietnam found there was a 'credibility gap' between what their politicians were telling them, and what they were seeing with their own eyes. They told their Government to pull out of Vietnam.

▽ During the Munich Olympics of 1972, terrorists took Israeli athletes hostage, and killed them. The events were reported world-wide on television. It was the first time that terrorists had hijacked the television system to publicise their demands.

▽ Until the 1980s, programmes had to hit as wide an audience as possible. The development of cable and satellite dishes has allowed dedicated channels for news (such as CNN), sport, shopping, pornography and children's programmes. Music Television (MTV) is aimed specifically at teenagers.

Beyond 2000

'THE PEOPLE'S CENTURY' has been a century of revolutions, fascism, oppression, depression, starvation and attempted genocide. More ordinary people have died in its wars than ever before.

Where will we go from here?

Few people nowadays see progress as automatic and inevitable.

How can this tiny planet feed its growing population? How can it provide the resources to give everybody the wasteful, Western standard of living they want? Will we destroy the world with pollution?

◁ Washington, 1992. Quilts stretching into the distance represent 20,000 people who have died of AIDS.

△ Women and children fetching water in India. In the future, water will be an increasingly important commodity.

How safe is democracy from nuclear war, terrorism and fanaticism? How safe are young people from drugs and alcohol?

Careless use of medicines has helped some diseases – such as tuberculosis – to become immune to modern medicines. There are new diseases such as AIDS which doctors cannot cure. Will scientists continue to be able to kill germs?

Or will your generation have to face a world of violence, hunger and disease?

IN 1969 MARJORIE BRANDT watched a man walking on the moon, live, on television. She says:

'I thought: my grandmother was in a log cabin and here I was seeing a man on the moon!'

That is the wonder of the 'People's Century'. It has been a time of democracy, plenty, and of medical and technological miracles.

Will things get better and better?

Will scientists find ways to give all nations adequate food,

heath and wealth? Will robots ever do the washing up or make the beds?

How many TV channels can we expect by the year AD 3000? The Internet 'superhighway' will provide any information we want, in our homes, at the press of a button. Can we look forward to a world where there is no more ignorance?

Will the United Nations grow in influence? Can we hope for an end to war, racism and political oppression?

Will your generation usher in a society of peace and plenty?

△ The world's expanding population is the biggest issue facing future generations. This poster from China is part of their one child per family campaign.

▽ You will be the history-makers of the next century.

Picture Credits

BBC Children's Books would like to thank the following for providing photographs and for permission to reproduce copyright material. While every effort has been made to trace and acknowledge all copyright holders, we would like to apologise should there have been any errors or omissions.

1 Hulton Deutsch, **2/3** Topham Picture Source, **6** ET Archive, **7** *(top)* Topham Picture Source, **7** *(bottom)* Topham Picture Source, **8/9** Peter Newark, **10/11** Peter Newark, **10** *(top and middle)* Bibliotheque des Arts Decoration, **11** *(top)* Raymond Abescat, **12** *(top)* ET Archive, **12** *(bottom)* Peter Newark, **13** Ann Ronan at Image Select, **14** *(top)* Peter Newark, **14** *(bottom)* Topham Picture Source, **15** Library of Congress, **16** Corbis-Bettman, **17** Library of Congress, **18** *(top)* National Library of Ireland, **18** *(bottom)* Library of Congress, **19** *(top)* Archivio Touring Club Italiano, **19** *(middle and bottom)* Ellis Island, **20** ET Archive, **21** *(top)* Corbis-Bettman, **21** *(middle)* Museum of Revolution, **23** *(middle)* ET Archive, **23** *(bottom)* AKG, **24** ET Archive, **25** *(top and middle)* AKG, **25** *(bottom)* Corbis-Bettman, **26** *(top and bottom)* ET Archive, **27** *(top)* Hermine Venot-Focké, **27** *(bottom left)* M. Batreau, **27** *(bottom, middle and right)* Walter Hare, **28** ET Archive, **29** *(top)* Peter Newark, **29** *(left)* David King Collection, **30/31** Advertising Archives, **32** *(top)* Hulton Deutsch, **32** (bottom) AKG, **33** *(top)* Karl Nagerl, **33** *(bottom)* AKG, **35** *(top)* Popperfoto, **35** *(bottom)* Hulton Deutsch, **36** *(top)* David King Collection, **36** *(bottom)* Hulton Deutsch, **37** BBC, **38** *(top)* Novosti London, **38** *(bottom)* David King Collection, **39** *(top)* Anastasia Denisova, **39** *(bottom)* David King Collection, **40** David King Collection, **41** Hulton Deutsch, **42** *(top)* Kobal Collection, **42** *(bottom)* Corbis-Bettman, **43** Ronald Grant Archive, **44** *(top)* Ronald Grant Archive, **44** *(bottom)* Kobal Collection, **45** BFI, **46** David King Collection, **47** *(top)* Huntley Film Archive, **47** *(bottom)* Popperfoto, **48** *(top)* NBC, **48** *(middle)* Imperial Tobacco Ltd., **48** *(bottom)* NBC, **49** Hulton Deutsch, **50** *(top and bottom left)* Anna Freund, **50** *(bottom right)* Corbis-Bettman, **51** *(top)* William Werber, **51** *(bottom)* NBC, **52** *(top, middle, bottom)* Ford Motor Company, **53** Fiat, **54** *(top)* Advertising Archives, **54** *(middle and bottom)* BFI, **55** *(top)* Giovanni Gobbi, **55** *(bottom)* Fiat, **56** (top) Bede Gallery, **56** *(bottom)* Corbis-Bettman, **57** *(top)* Henri Storck, **57** *(bottom)* Chilean Biblioteca Nacional, **58** *(top)* Swedish Labour Movement Archives, **58** *(bottom)* Corbis-Bettman, **59** *(top)* Loye Stoops, **59** *(bottom)* Corbis-Bettman, **60/61** AKG, **62/63** Hulton Deutsch, **62** *(top)* Hulton Deutsch, **63** *(top)* AKG, **64** AKG, **64** *(left and bottom)* AKG, **65** *(top)* Hanne-Lore Lügering, **65** *(right)* Ilse Woile, **65** *(bottom)* AKG, **66** *(top)* AKG, **66** *(middle)* YIVO Institute for Jewish Research, New York, **66** *(right)* Stadtarchiv Nuremberg, **67** AKG, **69** AKG, **70** *(left)* AKG, **70** *(top right)* Hulton Deutsch, **70** *(bottom)* Barnaby's Picture Library, **71** Peter Newark, **72** *(top)* Sid Newham, **72** *(middle)* Hulton Deutsch, **72/73** Hulton Deutsch, **73** *(middle)* AKG, **73** *(top right)* Margarete Slovioczek née Zettel, **74** AKG, **75** *(top and bottom)* Yad Vasham, **76** *(left)* David King Collection, **76** *(right)* Peter Newark, **77** *(top)* Lubov Zhakova, **77** *(bottom)* Leningrad Library, **78** *(top)* AKG, **78** *(bottom)* Corbis-Bettman, **79** Peter Newark, **82** (top) Hulton Deutsch, **82** (bottom) Keiko Saotome, **83** (left) Popperfoto, **83** (right) Hulton Deutsch, **84** *(top)* Hulton Deutsch, **84** (bottom) Peter Newark, **85** Hulton Deutsch, **86/87** Hulton Deutsch, **88** *(left)* David King Collection, **88** *(bottom)* Popperfoto, **89** (left) Corbis-Bettman, **89** *(right)* Hulton Deutsch, **90/91** Barnaby's Picture Library, **90** *(left)* Peter Newark, **90** *(right)* Raymond Jolivet, **91** *(right)* Hulton Deutsch, **92** Barnaby's Picture Library, **93** *(right)* Gail Halverson, **93** *(bottom)* AKG, **94** *(top)* Tamara Banketik, **94** *(bottom)* AKG, **95** *(top)* AKG, **95** *(bottom)* David King Collection, **96** *(top)* US National Archives, **96** *(bottom)* Corbis-Bettman, **97** (top) AKG, **97** *(bottom)* Peter Newark, **98/99** Corbis-Bettman, **98** *(left)* Corbis-Bettman, **99** *(top)* Alexei Kosmich Kondratiev, **100** Corbis-Bettman, **101** (top) AKG, **101** *(bottom)* Popperfoto, **102** *(top)* Birenda Kaur, **102** *(left and bottom right)* Hulton Deutsch, **103** Popperfoto, **104** *(left)* Hulton Deutsch, **104** *(right)* Popperfoto, **105** *(top)* Anim Assiful, **105** *(bottom)* Hulton Deutsch, **106** Hulton Deutsch, **107** *(top)* Popperfoto, **107** *(bottom)* Hulton Deutsch, **108** *(left, middle and right)* AKG, **109** *(top)* Advertising Archives, **109** *(bottom)* Corbis-Bettman, **110/111** Sally and Richard Greenhill, **112/113** *(bottom)* Corbis-Bettman, **112** *(top)* Corbis-Bettman, **113** *(top)* Hulton Deutsch, **114** *(top)* AKG, **114** *(right)* Popperfoto, **114** *(bottom)* Popperfoto, **115** *(top)* Ernest Green, **115** *(bottom)* Corbis-Bettman, **116** *(top)* Corbis-Bettman, **116** *(bottom)* Popperfoto, **117** Popperfoto, **118** *(top)* Popperfoto, **118** *(bottom)* Environmental Picture Library, **119** *(top)* Deborah Runkle, **119** *(middle)* Corbis-Bettman, **119** *(bottom)* Popperfoto, **120** *(top)* Duong Thanh Phong, **120** *(bottom)* Corbis-Bettman, **121** *(top)* Duong Thanh Phong, **121** *(bottom)* Hulton Deutsch, **122** *(top)* Barnaby's Picture Library, **122** *(bottom)* Corbis-Bettman, **123** *(top)* Hulton Deutsch, **123** *(bottom)* Corbis-Bettman, **124** *(top left)* London Features International, **124** *(bottom left)* Hulton Deutsch, **124** *(bottom right)* Retna, **125** *(top)* London Features International, **125** *(middle left, middle, middle right, bottom)* Retna, **126** *(top)* Environmental Picture Library, **126** *(bottom)* Popperfoto, **127** *(top)* Dusty Roads, **127** *(bottom)* Hulton Deutsch, **128** *(top)* Environmental Picture Library, **128** *(bottom)* AP/NASA, **129** *(top)* Environmental Picture Library, **129** *(bottom left)* Corbis-Bettman, **129** *(bottom right)* AP, **130** *(left and right)* Hulton Deutsch, **131** Hulton Deutsch, **131** *(inset)* Corbis-Bettman, **132** *(left)* Hulton Deutsch, **132** (right) Corbis-Bettmen, **133** *(top)* Popperfoto, **133** *(bottom)* Corbis-Bettman, **134** *(middle and bottom)* Corbis-Bettman, **135** *(top)* Corbis-Bettman, **135** (bottom) Popperfoto, **136** (top and bottom) Popperfoto, **137** (top and bottom) Popperfoto, **138** *(top)* Corbis-Bettman, **138** *(bottom left)* AKG, **138** *(bottom right)* Popperfoto, **139** *(top left)* Popperfoto, **139** *(top right)* Hubertus Kanus, **139** *(bottom left)* Corbis-Bettman, **139** *(bottom right)* Mirror Syndication International, **140/141** Environmental Picture Library, **140** *(top right)* Environmental Picture Library, **140** *(bottom left)* Corbis-Bettman, **141** *(top)* Environmental Picture Library, **141** *(bottom)* Pictor International.

Index